ANYONE FOR ORDINATION?

Anyone for Ordination?
A contribution to the debate on ordination

edited by

Paul Beasley-Murray

MARC
Tunbridge Wells

British Library Cataloguing in Publication Data
A catalogue record for this book is available
from the British Library

Cover design: Bene Imprimatur, Great Shelford

Production and Printing in England for
MARC, an imprint of Monarch Publications,
PO Box 163, Tunbridge Wells, Kent TN3 0NZ
by Indeprint, 13 Byne Road, London SE26 5JF

CONTENTS

CONTENTS

PREFACE

If there is one issue which above all divides the Christian church today, it is the issue of ordination. Thus in spite of certain maverick voices to the contrary, the Apostles' Creed is accepted by all the churches. In principle, at least, all Christians can happily confess their faith together. Where Christians and churches part company, however, is in their different understandings of the church and its ministry. This theological diversity finds its focus in questions relating to ordination: who may be ordained? why are people ordained? how should ordination take place? what happens in ordination?

For many people the issue of ordination came to the fore on 11th November 1992 with the Church of England's historic debate on the ordination of women. However, although Synod gave the green light for the ordination of women, this debate failed to resolve the issue. Indeed, whichever way the debate had gone, the issue would have been unresolved. The Church of England was and is split over who may be ordained to its ministry.

But the divisions over ordination are not peculiar to the Church of England. The Christian church as a whole is divided. Furthermore, these divisions do not simply relate to the issue of the ordination of women, but to the very nature of ordination itself.

All this came home to me when in 1982 the World Council of Churches published *Baptism, Eucharist and Ministry*, a document which had been through a number of drafts, but which received its final expression at the 1982 Faith and Order Conference meeting in Lima, Peru. Reading this document is a fascinating experience: there is a large measure of agreement

vii

here on baptism, but much less agreement on the subject of the eucharist, and even less agreement when it comes to ministry. Ministry – particularly the ordained ministry – is in fact the issue which divides churches, and hence which stops churches coming closer together.

Yes, perhaps surprisingly to some, it is neither the person of Christ nor the nature of the Trinity nor even the authority of the Scriptures which has proven the stumbling block to church unity. Indeed, in spite of much theological diversity, the World Council of Churches has defined itself as 'a fellowship of churches which confess the Lord Jesus Christ as God and Saviour according to the Scriptures, and therefore seeks to fulfil together their common calling to the glory of the one God, Father, Son and Holy Spirit'. Church unity instead founders above all on the differing understandings of ministry, differences which find their focus in ordination. The question of ordination is therefore no side-issue. It is the theological issue which the Christian church above all needs to attend to. Here then is to be found the relevance of *Anyone for Ordination?*

Since its publication in 1982 the mainline Christian denominations have made their official responses to *Baptism, Eucharist and Ministry*. For the most part these responses make pretty turgid reading. As I reflected on these responses, I realised that what was needed were people who could stimulate and stir the Christian constituency to take a fresh look at ministry and ordination, not least from a biblical perspective. It was this realisation which gave birth to this book. It is here that *Anyone for Ordination* has a special contribution to make.

My initial aim in compiling a symposium on ordination was to gain contributions from all the major strands of the British churches – Anglican and Roman Catholic, Free Church and 'New Church' (this last term is now commonly used for those charismatic streams formerly known as 'house churches'). To my delight, in this aim I have not been disappointed. As an examination of the contributors quickly reveals, I have been fortunate enough to gain a most impressive ecclesiastical spread. What is more, without exception my contributors are leaders of distinction. Perhaps their willingness to make time to contribute to this symposium in the midst of very busy lives, is an indication of the importance of the project. Certainly I wish to record my gratitude to them for their outstanding contributions to the debate.

One interesting result of this symposium is to discover that – as far as the present contributors are concerned – there appears to be an increasing convergence of opinion on the question of ordination and ministry. This is not to say that disagreements do not still remain – indeed, each essay reveals a quite distinctive perspective. However, in spite of all the differences there is for the most part a radical edge to their approach to the issue of ordination, which in turn surely poses a challenge to the Christian church as a whole.

Paul Beasley-Murray

THE CONTRIBUTORS

Paul Beasley-Murray read Modern Languages and Theology at Jesus College, Cambridge, before going on to Manchester, where alongside vocational training at the Northern Baptist College he gained a Ph.D. in New Testament studies from Manchester University. After further study at Zurich, he went to Zaire with the Baptist Missionary Society to teach in the Protestant Theological Faculty of the National University of Zaire. On his return he was for 13 years pastor of Altrincham Baptist Church, Cheshire, before being appointed in 1986 Principal of Spurgeon's College, a Baptist theological college in South London. In 1993 he returned to pastoral ministry as Senior Minister of Victoria Road South Baptist Church, Chelmsford, Essex. Co-author of *Turning the Tide* (Bible Society, London 1980), he has also written *Pastors under Pressure* (Kingsway, Eastbourne 1989), *Dynamic Leadership* (Marc/Monarch, Eastbourne 1990), *Faith and Festivity* (Marc/Monarch, Eastbourne 1991), and *Radical Believers* (Baptist Union, Didcot 1992).

Colin Buchanan read Classics at Oxford, before proceeding to be trained for Anglican ministry at Tyndale Hall, Bristol. In 1961, after three years as a curate in Cheadle, South Manchester, he joined the staff of the London College of Divinity, which later, on its move to Nottingham, became St John's College. Principal of St John's from 1979 to 1984, he was appointed Bishop of Aston in 1985. Now an assistant bishop in the diocese of Rochester, he is also serving as the vicar of St Mark's Gillingham. The founder, manager, and editor of the Grove Series of Booklets, he has for many years been at the forefront of liturgical renewal within the Church of England, editing such publications as *Modern Anglican Liturgies 1958–1968* (OUP, Oxford 1968), *Further Anglican Liturgies 1968–1975* (Grove Books, Bramcote 1968), *Latest Anglican Liturgies 1976–1984* (Alcuin/SPCK, London 1985), *Modern Anglican Ordination Rites* (Alcuin/GROW, London 1987), and *The Bishop in Liturgy* (Alcuin/GROW, London 1984). The joint editor of *Anglican Worship Today* (Collins, London 1980), he was joint author of *Growing into Union: Proposals for Forming a United Church in England* (SPCK, London 1970), and author of *Open to Others* (SU, London 1992).

Peter Cotterell studied physics and mathematics at Brunel University (B.Sc.), and theology at Spurgeon's College (Dip.Th.). After gaining a B.D. from London University, he went on to do a Ph.D. in Linguistics at the School of Oriental and African Studies and became a Fellow of the Institute of Linguistics. Missionary with the Sudan Interior Mission in Ethiopia 1957–1976, in 1976 he was appointed to the staff of London Bible College, of which he has been Principal since 1989. Author of 14 books, his publications include *Church Alive* (IVP, Leicester 1981), *This is Christianity* (IVP, Leicester 1985), *Cry Ethiopia* (Kingsway, Eastbourne 1988), *Mission and Meaninglessness* (SPCK, London 1990), and, with Max Turner, *Linguistics and Biblical Interpretation* (SPCK, London 1969).

Donald English read history at London University, and after taking a Diploma in Education at Leicester, was a Travelling Secretary with the Inter-Varsity Fellowship (now the Universities and Colleges Christian Fellowship). He has taught in theological colleges both in England and Nigeria, and is at present General Secretary of the Methodist Home Mission Division. The only person, since Methodist Union in 1932, to be twice elected President of the British Methodist Conference, he has also been Moderator of the Free Church Federal Council. At present he is Chairman of the World Methodist Council. He has written *God in the Gallery* (Epworth, London 1975), *Christian Discipleship* (Methodist Church Home Mission Division, London 1977), *Windows on the Passion* (Epworth, London 1978), *From Wesley's Chair* (Epworth, London 1979), *Everything in Christ* (Bible Reading Fellowship, London 1988), *Evangelism Now* (Methodist Church Home Mission Division, London 1988), and *The Message of Mark* (IVP, Leicester 1992).

Roger Forster graduated from St John's College, Cambridge, in mathematics and theology. He then worked as an itinerant evangelist until 1974, when he founded in South London the Ichthus Christian Fellowship, which he has led ever since. Among his many responsibilities he is one of the founders and directors of March for Jesus, one of Tear Fund's honorary vice-Presidents, and is on the international planning committee of the AD 2000 church-planting movement and also on the council of management of the Evangelical Alliance. He has written six books, which include *God's Strategy in Human History* (Highland Books, Crowborough 1989), *Reason and Faith* (Monarch, Eastbourne 1989), and *Finding the Path* (IVP, Leicester 1991).

Alan Kreider moved from Indiana to London in 1966 to study English history, which resulted in *English Chantries: The Road to Dissolution* (OUP, Oxford 1979). Remaining in England his interests developed into a search for forms of Christian mission, congregational life and social strategy appropriate to the post-Christian West. This search has been experimental (leadership in the Wood Green Mennonite Church, participation in Christian movements for peace, justice and the equality of women) and historical (participation in the Anabaptist Network, research on the life, worship, and social dynamics of early Christianity). Formerly he and his wife Eleanor were directors of the London Mennonite Centre. In 1991 they moved to Manchester, where they are 'Theologians-in-Residence' at the Northern Baptist College and where Alan teaches Ecclesiastical History part-time at the University of Manchester. A popular statement of his concerns is his *Journey Towards Holiness* (Marshall Pickering, London 1986).

Wilfrid McGreal, has been a Carmelite Friar since 1958. His university education took place in Rome, Dublin and Canterbury. An occasional lecturer at the Franciscan Study Centre in Canterbury, he has been much involved in Adult Education in the Christian world, whether as a Warden of Allington Castle or Prior at Hazlewood Castle, Tadcaster. Currently he is involved in an evangelizing ministry at Aylesford, Kent, as Director of Pilgrimages. He is also a contributor to religious programmes on the BBC.

R.J. ('Jack') McKelvey holds degrees from Nottingham (B.A.) Pittsburgh (M.Th.) and Oxford (D.Phil.). He was involved in theological education in Southern Africa for many years where he helped set up the Federal Theological Seminary of Southern Africa and the Theological Education by Extension College. Since his return to the UK in 1979 he has been Principal of Northern College, Manchester (United Reformed and Congregational) and has been intimately involved in the creation of the Northern Federation for Training in Ministry. His speciality is New Testament and his major work *The New Temple* (OUP, Oxford 1969) has become a standard reference text on the subject of the church from the aspect of the divine indwelling.

Vera Sinton is director of pastoral studies in Wycliffe Hall, Oxford. An Oxford mathematics graduate, she taught in Hong Kong and then worked for 8 years for the Universities and Colleges Christian Fellowship. After ordination training at

Trinity College, Bristol, she taught at All Nations Christian College, before returning to Oxford in 1987. She is a contributor to *Jesus 2000* (eds. R. Bauckham, R.T. France, M. Maggay, J. Stamoolis, C.P. Thiede, Lion, Tring 1989) and *Restoring the Vision* (ed. M. Tinker, Monarch, Eastbourne 1990) and author of *How Can I Forgive?* (Lion, Tring 1990).

1. Ordination in The New Testament

Paul Beasley-Murray

Introduction

'No Clergy in Paul's Letters' is one of the headings in Richard Hanson's *Christian Priesthood Examined* (Lutterworth, Guildford 1979). Such a slogan is but an echo of Ernst Käsemann, who in his influential paper 'Ministry and Community in the New Testament' (later published in *Essays in New Testament Themes*, SCM, London 1964, 63–94) argued that the New Testament has no technical definition of what we are accustomed to call ecclesiastical office.

Unfortunately such statements are one-sided. Important as it is to recognize the charismatic nature of the early Christian church, it is clear that, along with 'every-member-ministry', particular leadership roles were emerging. Such passages as Rom 16.1f and Phil 1.1 indicate that 'bishops' and 'deacons' were not the creation of a post-Pauline, post-charismatic church.

In this essay, however, we do not want to look at the large issue of 'ministry', but rather confine ourselves to investigating the way in which people were appointed to particular ministries: i.e. the intention of this paper is to study patterns of 'ordination' (if that not be too anachronistic a word) in the New Testament. With this in mind we shall examine five key passages: Acts 6.1–6; 13.1–3; 14.23; 1 Tim 4.14; 2 Tim 1.6.

Acts 6.1–6

The appointment of the Seven to free the apostles to concentrate on 'prayer and the ministry of the word' raises all sorts of questions:

1. Who are these Seven? Traditionally the Seven have been viewed as 'deacons', for their task is described in terms of 'serving tables' (*diakonein trapezais*). However, it is generally acknowledged that there is no justification for such an inference. The Greek word *diakonia* is a general term used to describe 'ministry' in general (see, e.g. 1 Cor 12.5; 2 Cor 5.18; Eph 4.12), and therefore does not refer to the service of 'deacons' in particular. All of the Seven in Acts 6 were men of spiritual distinction ('men known to be full of the Spirit and wisdom', 6.3). In particular, Stephen was a creative theologian (see Acts 7), and Philip a gifted evangelist (see Acts 8) – they were certainly no ordinary Baptist deacons! The nomenclature of the Seven indicates that they belonged to the Hellenist group within the early church, and we are probably right in assuming that they were already acting as leaders within that particular group. Indeed, there is much to be said for the suggestion that they were more akin to 'elders' rather than to 'deacons'.

2. What was the task of the Seven? What did Luke mean by 'serving tables'? Does 'serving tables' refer to the financial management of the common fund (the tables here then being bankers' tables)? The GNB, for instance, renders the phrase: 'handle finances'. Or does the term refer to the 'distribution of food (so the NIV) brought together perhaps at the daily 'agape'-meals (the equivalent of the Jewish 'poor basket')? Joachim Jeremias, *Jerusalem in the Time of Jesus*, SCM, London 1964, 131, favours the latter, drawing parallels with the Jewish system of relief (the so-called 'poor bowl' and the 'poor basket'). Certainty is impossible to obtain.

3. What was the role of the apostles in the appointment of

the Seven? It is clear that the apostles took the initiative in asking the church to 'choose seven men from among you who are known to be full of the Spirit and wisdom' (6.3). The selection of the Seven was therefore very much a church matter. However, what is not clear is whether it was the church as a whole or just the apostles who actually laid hands on the Seven. The Greek itself is somewhat vague: literally, 'these they set before the apostles, and having prayed they laid their hands upon them' (6.6). The NIV opts for the apostles: 'They presented these men to the apostles, who prayed and laid their hands upon them'. On the other hand, the more natural sense of the Greek would indicate that the whole church was involved in the laying on of hands, the subject of the verb 'they presented' being also the subject of the following verbs, 'and having prayed they laid their hands upon them'. True it may perhaps be objected that when first proposing the scheme, the apostles spoke of men 'whom we may appoint to this duty'. However, as David Daube, *The New Testament and Rabbinic Judaism*, Athlone Press, London 1956, 238, rightly argued, the ' "we" here most probably includes those whom they address; it means "we, the Christians of Jerusalem", not "we, the apostles"; it says nothing about the mode of installation'. If so, then there would be an Old Testament precedent in the mass-ordination of the Levites in Num 8.10. As we shall see, Acts 13.1−3 might well indicate that the church as a whole were involved in laying on of hands. Certainly, if the church as a whole were not all actively involved, one could well argue that the ceremony was under the direction of the church.

4. What happened when hands were laid on the Seven? It is often argued that in so far as the Seven are described as men already 'full of the Spirit and wisdom' (6.3), hands cannot have been laid upon them with a view to their being filled with the Spirit. Indeed, it was precisely because they were already 'full of the Spirit and wisdom' that they were chosen to deal with the problems arising from the growing number of widows in the church! Presumably, however, the very fact that the laying

3

on of hands was accompanied by prayer is an indication that such recognition does not rule out prayer for a further filling of the Spirit. As Luke in his account of the early church shows, there is nothing static about the Spirit (see Acts 4.8,31; also Eph 5.18). At the very least we can therefore say that along with a recognition of their spiritual gifts of leadership, prayer was also made that God would bless them in the new form of service they were about to undertake for him.

We may also infer that along with this act of recognition and prayer for blessing went also a commissioning to a particular task. The Seven were being set aside for a particular 'ministry'. Presumably implicit in that commissioning was also a conferring of authority. The church − or the apostles on behalf of the church − invested them with the authority necessary to discharge their special task. Here we enter into the complex debate as to whether hands were 'placed upon' the Seven for blessing or hands were 'leant upon' the Seven with a view to making them the formal representatives of the church (for a discussion of the Hebraic distinction between *sim/shith*, on the one hand, and *samakh*, on the other hand, see Daube, *The New Testament and Rabbinic Judaism* 224ff). The Greek itself gives no indication. However, it may well be that there is a parallel with the 'Seven of a City' elected by the Jewish inhabitants of a Palestinian city to look after the common affairs and who had the full power of representation. If this parallel is valid, as it would appear to be, then we could conclude that the church in setting apart the Seven made them their representatives and thus delegated to them something of its authority.

It should be emphasised that the whole process is very dynamic. It is unhelpful to talk of this action as being an 'institution to an office': the emphasis is on a service to be rendered, rather than upon an office to be entered upon. Certainly all talk of 'a special status' is unhelpful: there was a role to be fulfilled, not a dignity to be maintained. Again, it is anachronistic in seeing here an 'ordination' for 'life'. Eduard Schweizer, *Church Order in the New Testament*, SCM

4

London 1961, 25c, is right when he says: 'here men are "installed" for a quite definite ministry within the local church at Jerusalem, with no thought of any further activity beyond this definite task'.

Acts 13.1–3

A second passage in Acts often cited as a biblical precedent for ordination concerns the setting apart of Barnabas and Paul for missionary service.

The first question which arises is: who actually set Barnabas and Paul apart? The prophets and teachers, or the church as a whole? The Greek is unclear. Howard Marshall, *Acts*, IVP, Leicester 1980, 215, attractively argues: 'Since the list of names in vl is primarily meant to show who was available for missionary service, and since changes of subject are not uncommon in Greek, it is preferable to assume that Luke is thinking of an activity involving the members of the church generally; this will fit in with the fact that elsewhere similar decisions are made by the church as a whole (1.15; 6.2,5; cf 14.27; 15.22)'. If Marshall is right, then we may assume that it was within the context of a church worship service at which the Spirit spoke through one of the prophets, calling the church to put aside two of its leaders. This setting aside involved both the laying on of hands and prayer.

What was involved in this action of the laying on of hands and of prayer? In so far as Barnabas and Paul were already recognised leaders (i.e. they already belonged to the group of prophets and teachers), it could hardly have been an act of recognition of their leadership. Rather they are commissioned for a new sphere of service, for which prayer is then made. We may well envisage that prayer was offered for these two men to be empowered afresh with God's Spirit, in order that they might fulfil their mission. But did the laying on of hands involve more? Were hands simply 'placed' upon Paul and Barnabas for blessing (cf the Hebrew *sim/shith*), or were hands 'leant' upon Paul and Barnabas in order that they might become representatives of the Antioch church (cf the Hebrew *samakh*)? If there is an allusion to the consecration of the Levites in Numbers 8, then perhaps the latter is right: i.e. just as the Levites were 'set apart' from the other Israelites for special service, so too Paul and Barnabas were 'set apart' for special service. If this interpretation is right, then Paul and Barnabas, in being commissioned for service, were being sent out as representatives of the church of Antioch and were therefore invested with authority to act on behalf of that Christian community at Antioch.

There is no indication that Paul and Barnabas were being 'set apart' in terms of who they were, as distinct from what they were to do. This being 'set apart' is purely functional. True, as we have already seen in the Old Testament, the Levites were 'set apart' as priests, but there is no reason to assume that Paul and Barnabas by virtue of prayer with laying on of hands become some separate priestly caste. This is not ordination in the sense that there Paul and Barnabas are given a new status. Eduard Schweizer, *Church Order in the New Testament*, 24c, is therefore on firm ground when he argues that 'It is not a matter of ordination . . . It is an "installation" ' to a particular task.

Acts 14.23

Luke in his description of Paul's first missionary journey tells how in Derbe, Lystra, and Iconium, 'Paul and Barnabas appointed elders for them in each church'.

There has been much dispute as to the historicity of this account. James Dunn, *Jesus and the Spirit*, SCM, London 1975, 182, for instance, writes: 'Luke suggests that Paul followed the Jerusalem pattern by appointing elders in his churches (14.23; 20.17); but we have absolutely no confirmation of this from Paul himself'. It is true that, with the exception of the Pastorals, Paul never uses the word 'elder' for a church leader. However, as F.F. Bruce, *Acts*, Eerdmans, Grand Rapids, 2nd ed 1988, p. 280, rightly argued, 'The

6

language may be Luke's but it is plain from Paul's letters that he made provision for spiritual guidance in the churches which he founded and encouraged the members to recognize and respect their leaders' (cf 1 Cor 16.15–18; Gal 6.6; Phil 1.1; 2.29; 1 Thess 5.12–13). C.K. Barrett, *Church, Ministry and Sacraments in the New Testament*, Paternoster, Exeter 1985, 52, somewhat quaintly makes the same point: 'It would not . . . be wide of the mark to say that what Luke means in his use of the word is that when Paul took leave of the churches . . . he said to his earlier and best trusted converts (cf 1 Cor 16.15), "Please keep an eye on things for me till I return", and that such people were, in Luke's day and in the churches known to him, described as presbyters (elders)'. Whatever the name, therefore, Paul certainly appointed leaders.

But what was involved in such an appointment? Interest has centred around the verb Luke uses, *cheirotoneo*, which in later ecclesiastical usage came to mean 'to impose hands in ordination'. However, in the secular usage of the day it simply meant 'to appoint'. Originally the verb referred to 'raising the hand to express agreement in a vote', but there is no indication that in Acts 14 the churches were involved in the election of their leaders. Thus whereas in 2 Cor 8.19 we read that a representative was chosen (*cheiroteneitheis*) by 'the churches' to accompany Paul on his journey to take the collection to Jerusalem, at this embryonic stage of church life Paul and Barnabas took the initiative in 'appointing' or 'installing' the new leaders. As Eduard Schweizer, *Church Order in the New Testament*, 23c, rightly comments, the fact that leaders were appointed with no reference to the church is exceptional and is simply 'a question of newly formed churches . . . Elsewhere, however, the Church has a vital share in important choices and decisions, and takes the final responsibility'. It may well be that this appointment involved the laying on of hands. Certainly the reference to 'prayer and fasting' is reminiscent of the occasion when Barnabas and Saul were set apart 'after fasting and prayer' (13.3). As for the content of the prayer, we read 'they committed them to the Lord in whom they had put their trust' (cf 20. 32). Within the context of 14.22f ('We must go through many hardships to enter the kingdom of God') a prayer for protection would have been quite natural. Whether or not it included a prayer for an empowering with God's Spirit is not known.

1 Tim 4.14

The situation appears to be somewhat analogous to that of Acts 13.1–3, where the Spirit spoke apparently through one of the prophets. Just as at Antioch the Spirit had caused the church to set aside Paul and Barnabas for missionary service, so here the Spirit through the voice of prophecy caused Timothy to be set aside for the ministry of preaching and teaching. Thus the Revised English Bible translates: 'Do not neglect the spiritual endowment given you when, *under the guidance of prophecy*, the elders laid their hands upon you'. It was on the basis of the Spirit-inspired utterances that the elders set Timothy aside. The laying on of hands was the church's response to the Spirit's initiative (see also 1 Tim 1.18, where Paul writes: 'Timothy, my son, I give you this instruction ('charge') in keeping with the prophecies once made about you').

It is important too to emphasize that the Spirit and his gifts are still conceived in dynamic terms here in the Pastorals. *Charisma* ('gift') is not, as James Dunn, *Jesus and the Spirit* 348, would suggest, 'the power of office'. *Charisma* here is more akin to the ministries of Eph 4.11 ('apostles, prophets, evangelists, pastor-teachers'), which are perceived gifts of the Ascended Christ. This dynamism comes to expression in the way in which vv13f of 1 Tim 4 parallel one another: to devote oneself to reading the Scriptures in public, to preaching and to teaching, is in fact not to neglect one's gift.

Who laid hands upon Timothy? The English versions imply that the elders did. However, according to David Daube, *The New Testament and Rabbinic Judaism* p. 224f, we have here a rabbinic expression which should be translated, 'when hands were laid upon you with the object of making you into an elder'! However, such a suggestion produces a most unnatural meaning of the Greek phrase. It is more natural to accept the normal translation: 'when the body of elders laid their hands upon you'. The difficulty with this customary translation is that there then appears to be a contradiction with 2 Tim 1.6, where Paul only talks of himself laying hands on Timothy. However, in 2 Tim 1.6 Paul is not seeking to assert that he alone laid hands upon Timothy. Paul may simply have 'presided' over Timothy's setting apart, just as in an ordination of a Rabbi the candidate was ordained by his teacher with the co-operation of two assistants. The apparent differences can therefore be easily harmonized.

2 Tim 1.6

At the beginning of his second letter to Timothy Paul writes, 'Fan into flame the gift of God, which is in you through the laying on of my hands'. If 1 Tim 4.14 be any guide, then this verse does not refer to baptism, which was often accompanied by the laying on of hands (see Heb 6.2; Acts 9.17), but to the occasion when Timothy was set aside for ministry as a preacher-teacher.

In Tim 4.14 the gift in question was the gift of the ministry of preaching and teaching, but here in 2 Tim 1.6 the gift is seen primarily in terms of the Spirit himself. The implication is that Timothy had experienced a special outpouring of the Spirit. Timothy has received not just authority, but also quite distinct blessing. Now, rather than quenching the Spirit through his natural timidity, Paul encourages him to step out in faith and allow the Spirit full rein in his life. Indeed, this stepping out is to be a continuous process: or to use Paul's metaphor, it involves a constant fanning of the flame. No pastor can rely on past experience. In the words of the Anglo-Catholic scholar, J.N.D. Kelly, *The Pastoral Epistles*, Black, London 1963, 159: 'If ordination is already regarded as imparting a positive grace, the idea that this grace operates automatically is excluded. The

Christian minister must be continually on the alert to revitalise it'. As in 1 Tim 4.14, the emphasis is on the sovereign activity of the Spirit. The laying on of hands is never in itself causal. No individual or group of individuals can ever control or manipulate the Spirit!

As we have already argued, almost certainly the reference here to Paul's hands is not intended to be exclusive. To quote Gordon Fee, *1 & 2 Timothy and Titus*, Hendrickson, Massachusetts 1984, 226, 'In 1 Tim 4.14, where a part of the concern was to authenticate Timothy before the church, Paul mentions the laying on of hands by the elders. Here, where the interest is almost totally personal, the focus is on Paul's own part in that call, thus appealing to their close personal ties'.

Conclusions

1. All five passages examined suggest that in the churches of the New Testament leaders were normally appointed with prayer and with the laying on of hands. In this regard the appointment of the leaders of the young church had much in common with the appointment of Jewish rabbis. Although there may be no hermeneutical principle which necessitates that particular custom be normative in today's church, there does seem much to be said in maintaining this symbolic act of solidarity and prayer.

2. All five passages examined clearly indicate that leaders in the churches of the New Testament were not self-appointed. The evidence, however, is not so clear as to how they were appointed. In two of the five passages (Acts 6 and Acts 13) leaders were appointed either by or under the direction of the local church. On the other hand, in the Pastoral Epistles the role of the church receives no mention: there hands are laid upon Timothy by the elders (1 Tim 4.14) – a ceremony in which Paul took a particular part (2 Tim 1.6). Likewise in Acts

14.23 elders were appointed by Paul and Barnabas apparently without reference to the church — but in so far as the churches in Lystra, Iconium and Antioch were only at an early stage of their life, it may fairly be argued that this was exceptional (was this also the situation envisaged in Titus 1.5?). Certainly if other evidence of the role of the church is taken seriously (see, for instance, Mt 18.15—20; Acts 15.22,28; 1 Cor 5.4f), then it may well be that the silence of the Pastorals regarding the role of the church is not unduly significant — it may be that their role is simply assumed. Whatever the truth may be, the principle underlying the doctrines of the priesthood of all believers (1 Pet 2.4f,9: see also 1 Tim 2.5) and of the ministry of all believers (see, for instance, 1 Cor 12) would encourage the practice today of involving the local church as a whole in the appointment of their leaders.

3. Both Acts and the Pastoral Epistles underline the necessity for leaders to be appropriately gifted and of good character. In Acts 6, for instance, the church at Jerusalem is told to choose seven men 'known to be full of the Spirit and of wisdom'. In Acts 13 Paul and Barnabas had already proved themselves as leaders in the church at Antioch before they were appointed for missionary service. If 1 Tim 3.1—7 and 2 Tim 2.2 (see also 1 Tim 4.12) be any guide, then Timothy will already have evidenced good character as well as the ability to teach before being set apart.

4. Although leaders of the New Testament churches appear to have exercised authoritative (see Heb 13.17; 1 Thess 5.12; 1 Tim 1.3,5; 4.11; 5.7) — as distinct from authoritarian (see 1 Pet 5.2f) — leadership, it is not clear from the passages we have examined whether authority as such was specifically delegated to them in the ceremony of laying on of hands. Much rests upon the rabbinic evidence, which David Daube adduces. If Daube is right, then in Acts 6 and Acts 13 hands were laid upon the Seven and upon Paul and Barnabas not just with a view to conferring blessing, but also with a view to delegating authority to them to enable them to discharge their duties in

the name of the church. With the rabbinic practise in mind, in 1 Tim 4.1 the emphasis is probably upon the authority received by Timothy to discharge his ministry of preaching and teaching, whereas in 2 Tim 2.6 the emphasis is upon the blessing received. As for today's practise, few people involved in ordination services would have any awareness of the Hebrew distinction between 'placing hands upon' and 'leaning hands upon' particular individuals. Nonetheless, there are important implications. For in ordination the church is not simply recognizing a person as called of God to leadership, it is also at the same time delegating the authority necessary for them to fulfil their ministry. Such authority is held 'in trust' and as such has an element of accountability built into it — those whom God has called and the church has recognized are accountable both to the Lord (see Heb 13.17; Jas 3.1) as also to the church (see esp Matt 18.15–20).

5. Three of the passages examined suggest that leaders in the churches of the New Testament were appointed to a particular task rather than to a generalized form of service in the church as a whole. Thus in Acts 6 and Acts 13 both the Seven and Paul and Barnabas were appointed to fulfil a specific function, as were presumably the elders in Acts 14. In the Pastorals the picture is less clear: did Timothy receive authority for a particular situation or for a particular ministry? Maybe the question is not real: for if Acts is to be believed, Timothy's ministry was not limited to Ephesus, but was wider in view. In this regard Timothy's appointment is more akin to ordination today, where ordination to a leadership ministry is to be distinguished from induction to a particular situation.

6. Finally, on a negative note, at no stage is priestly language used of the appointment of leaders, as if the leaders of the churches in the New Testament were perceived as possessing a special status — as distinct from function — in the church. Thus we observed in Acts 13.2, that although Luke speaks of Paul and Barnabas being 'set apart', it is very much a

functional being 'set apart': i.e. it was first and foremost with a view to being 'sent off' on a missionary journey that Paul and Barnabas were 'appointed'. On reflection, the language of being 'set apart' at ordination is unhelpful, for it can imply that those being ordained are no longer part of the people of God, but belong to a separate order.

2. The threefold order in question
An Anglican perspective

Colin Buchanan

To write on a theology of ordination is to walk into a kind of deadly trap – a kind of theological catch 22. It is said that a man ran a toll-gate in America. When he got bored with collecting dollars he started a different plan – he stopped each driver and asked him, instead of paying, to make a statement. When the driver did so, the toll-gateman judged whether the statement was true or not – and he let through those who, in his judgement, spoke truth, and rejected those who did not. Then one day there came along a driver who, on being asked to make a statement, said 'You are not going to let me through this gate.' Now was that true or not? What were the implications of its perceived truth or deceitfulness? So is everyone who would write about orders. Any statement he makes will, if deemed true, probably lead him into a situation which falsifies his premise – and thus disqualifies him from being there: Furthermore the Church of England, in the name of which I write (though without charter from its authorities), has for over a century and a half had a fascination with the issue of ordination, to such a point that, even to write down the issue's importance is, by the sheer space given to that writing, to increase the fascination.

14

Historical Outline

The Church of England claims continuity from the pre-Reformation Church in England. The continuity can still be seen in our medieval churches and cathedrals, the feudal patronage of the Lord of the Manor, the actual provinces, dioceses, archdeacons and parishes of our organization, and a thousand other ways. At the time of the Reformation, the reform was (for all sorts of good reasons, including sheer accident of history) engineered 'from above'. Parliamentary Acts in Henry VIII's reign cut off the whole organization from Rome, and brought it, by an expropriation and nationalization process, under the monarch of England: and parliamentary Acts in Edward VI's reign brought to this now nationalized industry sweeping doctrinal and liturgical reform.

What was the role of the ordained ministers in this two-stage revolution? It is not hard to discern. From the Archbishop of Canterbury (Cranmer) downwards, each needed to assert his existing ordination and actual offices in order both to promote and to enjoy the reforms as they were being implemented. An Archbishop of Canterbury who called in question his own ordination, on the grounds that it had been popish, would have lost all authority to push forward the Reformation, and would thus have cut off the branch on which he was sitting. A parish priest (we shall come back to that word) who doubted his ordination would have been out of office and useless for furthering the reformed cause. Inevitably – and virtually without reflection – the Church of England clergy expressed confidence in their orders and their appointed offices, even when these had been received before the Reformation or at an early stage in it. The Church of England was committed to an outward stability, a visible continuity of its own life, even when a most sweeping reformation was being concluded within that life.

The first reformed and vernacular ordination rites were authorized in 1550. These printed before the liturgical texts the famous 'Preface to the Ordinal':

> *'It is evident unto all men, diligently reading holy scripture, and ancient authors, that from the Apostles' time, there hath been those orders of ministers in Christ's Church, Bishops, Priests and Deacons . . . And therefore to the intent that these orders should be continued, and reverently used and esteemed in this Church of England, it is requisite that no man . . . shall execute any of them, except he be called . . . and admitted, according to the form hereafter following.'*

It has become a *locus classicus* of one part of the Church of England to rest an enormous theological weight upon that one word 'continued'. We have seen above the relative (if accidental) inevitability of continuing offices called 'bishops' 'priests' and 'deacons'. It was *a priori* likely that such ministers should have similar roles and authority within the church-structured Tudor society that the previous ones had had – so that the parish priest, whether ordained in Henry's Roman Catholic days, or Henry's later Henrician Catholic days, or in Edward's first three years (when the Reformation was being pursued, but ordinations were still conducted by the Sarum Pontifical) or Edward's latter three years (when the Reformation was further advanced, and ordinations were conducted by the 1550, or even the later 1552, ordinal), was still the parish priest, in charge of the building, the liturgy, and the souls of his parishioners. The task might be re-expounded for him, and he would have to go along with that re-exposition or suffer penalties, but the framework of the task, deriving from his ordination, remained steadfastly in place. It was indeed the very means by which the Reformation was to come to the ordinary people – as the parish priest himself was reformed by parliamentary and comparable instructions from above.

Thus it was that 'these orders of Ministers in Christ's Church' were to be 'continued' according to the Preface to the Ordinal. They were, however, ruthlessly re-expounded. Even the 180 degree swingabout in the understanding of communion in Edward's reign hardly rivals the root and branch re-exposition of the nature of ordination and of the task of ministry deriving from it. The whole sacerdotal edifice of the medieval period came tumbling down, and a new 'ministry of God's word and sacraments' was built in its place. The pre-Reformation understanding had concentrated on the eucharist (with some side-reference to the sacrament of penance) – and in particular therefore on the priesthood, and the powers of the priest, and the task of 'offering sacrifices on behalf of the living and the dead'. All that now went, and its departure was graphically symbolized in the two-stage shift in the *porrectio* at the ordination – from the giving of paten and chalice in Sarum, to the giving of paten and chalice with a Bible in 1550, to the giving of the Bible alone in 1552. By 1552 the rite was saturated with references to the ministry of the word, and the ministry of the sacraments (two ordinances only being viewed as sacraments) was clearly subordinate to the ministry of the word, simply underlining and reinforcing that which was primarily given by the word. The ordination rites and their understanding of ordained ministry were unqualifiedly Protestant and evangelical.

From the middle of the sixteenth to the middle of the seventeenth centuries, Anglicans had a relatively relaxed apologia for episcopacy as over against other reformed patterns of ministry. Episcopal ordination, whilst ordered for the Church of England as we have seen, and whilst defended against the Puritans as more ancient and more appropriate than Presbyterian ordination, was not viewed as the sole Christian means of ordination, and presbyters from abroad, even if ordained Presbyterians, could be not only recognized, but received into the Church of England's ministry. It was only when attacks upon episcopacy at home grew intense, and as in Stuart times the doctrine of the Divine Right of Kings was expounded as founded upon episcopal church government, that the claims for episcopacy got higher and more exclusive. Then in the 1662 ordination rites, the Preface from 1550 was slightly retouched so as to require invariable episcopal ordination. There was a vengeful approach by the returning Royalists after the Restoration, and they vented their antagonism by requiring

17

all ministers left over from the Commonwealth period, if they had not been ordained by a bishop, now to submit to such ordination as though they had not been previously ordained at all.

So the threefold orders of ministry lived on in the Church of England, bound in with an aristocratic view of society and naturally wielding or influencing the levers of political power. The Methodist Revival was not a protest against the threefold orders (for all that John Wesley believed that to be a presbyter and to be a bishop were one and the same thing − and acted accordingly). It was rather a spiritual rising up against the existent arid regime in parish after parish, and a protest against the parish boundaries being used by the parson as self-protection against new spiritual life.

A different dawn came with the Oxford Movement from July 1833 onwards. Now, as the state props of the establishment started to buckle and fall away, John Keble asked the question in his Assize Sermon 'On what does our authority depend?' His answer was 'Upon the Apostolic Succession of Bishops', and this was followed up by Newman in Tract no. 1 (and in many other Tracts) saying 'We should not consider anyone to be truly ordained who is not *thus* ordained'. Episcopacy and the threefold orders were now basic to the very being a Christian Church at all − 'Catholic' orders were of the very *esse* of its being.

It can be argued that his view was entrenched in the 'Chicago-Lambeth Quadrilateral' of 1886 (and the 1888 Lambeth Conference), when the requirement of an agreed pattern of ministry was set out as the fourth leg of the 'Quadrilateral', with clear hints that only the threefold order would fulfil it. As a *sine qua non* of reunion, it went beyond anything in the Prayer Book or Thirty-Nine Articles, and had an exclusive ring in relation to non-episcopal churches.

It has been impossible to provide a single over-arching statement of *the* Anglican doctrine or ordination. I go on to explore some propositions intended at least to bring the question into manageable proportions.

Proposition One

The church is logically and theologically prior to any question of 'orders'.

The salvation of a company of people in Christ is prior to any form of appointment to any office in the people of God. One of the most significant agreements involved in the team of which I was one who twenty-two years ago wrote *Growing into Union* (Colin Buchanan, E. L. Mascall, J. I. Packer *Growing into Union: Proposals for Forming a United Church in England*, SPCK London 1970) was that the chapter on the church and sacraments should precede the one on episcopacy and ministry. Church first – ordination and ministry as a function of and within an already existing church. 'Ministry' itself, of course, as a translation of *diakonia* (otherwise rendered 'service'), obviously exists within the church as an informal function of mutual internal relations and also of activity to the world outside the church independently of, and in logical priority to, any question of ordination and 'orders'. I may add in passing that one of the several objections to the passing fancy there has been in fairly recent years of calling confirmation the 'ordination of the laity' is that it is logically fatuous. (There are other objections – particularly in what it implies for the meaning of baptism – but they are not germane to this essay.) The formal problem I am raising is that the ministry of the laity (to which, in this account of confirmation, the candidates are to be 'ordained') is more basic in the life of the church – it is actually theologically prior to the appointing of any laypersons by a process known as 'ordination' for certain specified purposes within the church. The concept of 'ordination' has no meaning prior to that, and thus it cannot possibly be the key to understanding the call to service of the people of God generally. So it is a logical absurdity – perhaps even an endless circle – rather like Cranmer's insistence that matrimony was instituted to avoid fornication, which suggests that logically fornication came first and matrimony was a contrived remedy to save the situation.

But fornication cannot come first, as its own definition must spring from a prior knowledge of what constitutes marriage. Similarly then the church and the ministry of the whole church are logically prior to the appointment of special persons and the allocation to them of specially defined powers, roles, or duties.

Proposition Two

Discussions of orders and ordination are bound to rely heavily upon the descriptive *use of language.*

This is saying that each work in this field has simply described *how* the institution of ordained ministry has worked or developed in history. Thus, to give but one example, in the ARCIC 1 statement on 'Ministry and Ordination' phrases constantly recur such as 'Both presbyters and deacons are ordained by the bishop' (16), 'the evidence suggests that with the growth of the church the importance of certain functions led to their being located in specific officers of the community' (5). These statements and a dozen other ones are simply of the form 'this is apparently what happened'. We have an inherited pattern of ordinations – yes, and, if you like, of 'orders' – and the only sanction we can claim for it is 'this is the way it turned out'. If you look carefully at the second quotation I raised you will see three things are being said:

(i) we have no command of our Lord, no New Testament prescription, for there to be stated kinds of officers in the church, let alone for them to fulfil certain functions.

(ii) the church as a whole is said to be the original repository of the 'certain functions', which it then located with 'specific officers'.

(iii) whether the officers antedated the locating of functions with them, or whether they were newly created for the purpose, is not entirely clear.

20

Of course, we need to have a positive doctrine of tradition. We need to see tradition as properly conveying God-given truth. We need to give it *prima facie* credibility. But we also need to assess it, evaluate it, judge it, and reform it, if it clashes with God's truth, or inhibits his mission on earth.

Proposition Three

Behind the historical phenomena the New Testament is very hard to probe.

To be accurate, we can state that is very hard to probe in such a way that it gives off lessons for us. I offer a cluster of homespun wisdoms in relation to this:

(i) *homespun wisdom number one:* we go to the New Testament for principles of *leadership*, which we are fairly sure is one of the integral features of church officers − though not confined to the ordained. Thus in 1 Peter 5, we learn about not lording it over the flock of God. We may not draw a short straight line from Peter's *presbuteroi* (who were also *episkopoi*) to the 'presbyters' of the ARCIC report, but you can reckon that principles of leadership set out in the New Testament may actually bear upon Christian leaders today. That does not touch the 'orders' question, of course.

(ii) *homespun wisdom number two;* there is a hauntingly interesting article by a Roman Catholic, Douglas Powell, *'Ordo Presbyterii,' Journal of Theological Studies* 26 (1975) 290−328, in which he contends that 'presbyter' is used in the New Testament church of those who are senior *in the faith* − and it is therefore a status-word, not a function-word like 'bishop' and 'deacon'. That would explain why the word can be used interchangeably with 'bishop'. It does not preclude recognition or accreditation, but it creates a general class within which the bishops and deacons had specific roles, presumably. Powell goes on to work out how this may have developed into second century patterns.

(iii) *homespun wisdom number three:* there is in the New Testament no discernible link between leadership of the flock in general, and what we would call liturgical leadership. Here again, we shall be dependent upon what actually happened to discover a doctrine or a discipline. We may argue a congruity, but we have to acknowledge the gaps in the argument. And, infuriatingly, in Corinth, where it appears that there was disorder at both the bring-your-own-grub sacramental feast (1 Cor 11), and the bring-your-own-gift verbal celebration (1 Cor 14), in neither place – nor elsewhere in the whole letter – does Paul address any responsible church officers to tell them to pull things into shape. He does use that famous verse 'Let all things be done decently and in order' – almost the only verse in 1 Corinthians 14 known to the Church of England (though it is of course a foundational document of the whole life of the Church of England), but even that verse suffers from our point of view in that it gives commands in the passive – 'all things be done' – so no assigning of any identifiable responsibility to any leaders can be elicited from it. Word and sacraments may be constitutive of the origins and continuance of the church (I believe they are), but any link with church officers remains tenuous and inferential, and is far short of clinching any argument.

Proposition Four

If we are driven to history, then to gain any assurance we shall have to affirm both that we know what has happened, and also that 'what is, is right'.

This, to put it another way, amounts to 'what has developed, has developed right', or even 'what is, must be'. And here the slide over from the descriptive into the prescriptive want watching. I do not say it should not be done – I only say that a scrupulous view of history (and especially the inconvenient parts) must come first, and the slide from what has been to what must be must itself then find clear justification.

22

Let us then look at some history to get our knowledge of it clear. I offer some knobbly bits:

(i) *knobbly bit one:* the very first bit of history simply is not there. I had the bright idea of looking up an essay written nearly forty years ago by someone not particularly of my own theological persuasion – it was in fact by Hugh Montefiore, the then vice-principal of Westcott House, Cambridge. In his essay entitled 'The Historic Episcopate' (to be found in Kenneth Carey (ed) *The Historic Episcopate in the Fulness of the Church*, Dacre Press 1954, 110–111, he wrote, with reference to the origins of the ordained ministry:

'The evidence of the New Testament itself is too scattered, inconclusive, and even inconsistent. Our knowledge of the sub-apostolic period is equally fragmentary and uncertain. From the nature of the evidence there can be no clear proof . . .'

He then writes of:

'. . . the stir caused by the publication of *The Apostolic Ministry*. This is partly due to its massive facade of scholarship, partly to extravagant claims which accompanied it . . . In fact, it is open to damaging criticism: but, however brilliantly it was propounded, it could never attain to more than probability . . . Probability is not enough.'

Conclusion of knobbly bit one: history is undemonstrable on this vital point.

(ii) *knobbly bit two:* although the names 'bishop', 'presbyter' and 'deacon' are used from the time of Ignatius of Antioch onwards, they were nothing like our perception of them. Indeed they looked more like a vicar, a PCC, and a curate. There was nothing like our episcopacy, which may have oversight of up to 600 parishes on the Church of England scene – or up to a million square miles on the Australian. And the presbyterate was a kind of governing council in the local church, with the bishop presiding over it, whilst the deacon was the personal assistant to the bishop.

(iii) *knobbly bit three:* although there was a concern for 'succession' in the second century, it seems to have been related to an open succession of teachers in office, not to a quasi-sacramental method of conferring powers on them. In other words, Irenaeus opposes the Marcionites, Valentinians, and Basilideans, because he can demonstrate that they are mid-century johnny-come-latelies, whereas by contrast there is an open succession of orthodox teachers going back to the apostles, a succession in which he took his own place, having learned from Polycarp, who sat at the feet of John, who was a disciple of Christ. In days when there were not printed Bibles in the homes, nor available in the shops, the minister was the embodiment of the word of God. To find the word of God, one had recourse to the bishop. We may be back near to that today – in areas of practical illiteracy learning by heart, and handing on the tradition in song and spoken liturgical text, are comparable to the handing on of the faith in the early centuries. But *we* are not near to the point where all bishops agree with each other – and in saying that I am not referring to internal disagreements of the bishops in the Church of England – but rather to the existence of all kinds of bishops with impeccable dynastic qualifications, but great disagreement on many issues from many denominations. If I may quote from Arthur Couratin (and therefore make an impeccable High Church statement) 'succession in the second century was more about bottoms on thrones than about hands on heads'.

(iv) *knobbly bit four:* how *can* we pass from saying 'the ordained ministry and the rites of ordination in fact developed this way' to saying 'this kind of ordained ministry is in fact prescribed by God for his church in an exclusive way for ever'? We in the Church of England did something in the sixteenth century for which there was no precedent – and you and I in effect subscribe to it. The Church of England broke off from the communion of the Church of Rome, and snapped its fingers at the Pope's excommunication. Until 1054 everybody had known that the whole church, to be catholic, had to be in communion with itself throughout. Then East and West in differing ways came to terms with the *de facto* split, though each retained the principle internally of being in communion with itself. Then in the sixteenth century the Church of England took the view that that which had been was not necessarily that which had to be. We have considered the question as to whether the ordained ministry truly was being 'continued' either was, or was intended to be, the same in substance, or function, as the medieval ordained ministry. The titles remained, the existent clergy remained in the parishes, but the ordination rites were disembowelled and re-embowelled, and that has to be recognized.

Some concluding questions

I go from my propositions to a series of questions arising from the data we have been examining. I can do no more than sketch them here, but am ready for at least the next stage in the argument if counter-questions are raised.

(i) *Orders and ontology:* once we enter the area of appointing officers for life, then we raise questions about their status when and as they are not fulfilling their functions. In a sense this goes right back to Clement's letter to the Corinthians in the 90s A.D. – but that refers to putting them out of their particular ministries, and does not actively discuss whether they have indelible orders or not. The medievals systematized, and incorporated the Thomist description that some sacraments confer a 'character' – a stamp or seal, which marks you for life (and, in some theories, for eternity) as a bishop, presbyter or deacon. This metaphysical mark logically precedes any fulfilling of functions – and outlives any relinquishing of them. Such an ontology protects the minister from any suggestion that he can fall in or out of orders, and thus protects the laity from any suspicion that, if he is morally dubious or failing at his job, then the sacraments he celebrates will be spurious. Indeed if the word 'orders' means anything it means something ontological. At root it is saying something important about God, about his church, and about his call to individuals – but it has come out clumsily, and sounds like a dollop of grace given to the individual, which is somehow inalienably his whatever he does. By far the most imaginative and appealing re-handling of this that I have come across is in the last chapter of Eric Mascall's *Theology and the Gospel of Christ*, (SPCK London 1977). The restatement of ontology there is put (admittedly speculatively) in relational terms – the ontology subsists in a determined relationship to the structures of the church, not in some change within the being of the individual. Insofar as I can attach any value to ontological ways of thinking, I find this a far more satisfactory line of enquiry than most. I would like to think that it arises from some seminal matters in the aforesaid *Growing into Union*, where we compared the 'historic ministry' to the bone-structure of the body.

(ii) *Orders and validity:* any once-for-all-for-life rite must lead us into concepts of validity, and this crosses again with ontology. It has in fact become a norm of classic theology to distinguish concepts of 'validity' from those of 'grace' – this being well known in the case of baptism, and indeed the background to sermons I find myself preaching at confirmations. It has surfaced in relation to ordination through history – the so-called Augustinian theory of orders (actually a construct on what Augustine said about Donatist baptism, I believe) could allow that some orders were valid beyond the borders of the catholic church – though of course they would lack grace. Thus orders could be conferred in historic linear descent, even without their being in the context of acknowledged catholic church life. Arguably the Church of England acted on this principle in Elizabeth's reign, when bishops were appointed and consecrated without any by-your-leave to the Pope, and possibly without much actual consent of the people. The bishops were bishops because they were ordained by undoubted bishops. We ourselves may be caught with this analysis when we meet *episcopi vagantes* and their presbyters and deacons. The opposite notion has marked our dealings with Presbyterianism and similar denominations – there we have been likely to say that the particular denomination's orders were owned by God, were blessed by his grace, were genuinely useful, but (*sotto voce*) were not actually valid!. There is some fairly demanding mapwork still to be done in this jungle, but I suspect we do actually still have to live in it, and should not wish to escape. If that is so, then we certainly need more and defter mapwork. If we were to go on to Roman Catholic views of Anglican orders, then we would be saying to Roman Catholics 'however doubtful you are about our ecclesiality, you know that you do not have to believe it to be above suspicion for you, *on your own Augustinian premises*, to recognize our orders as historically sustained and actually valid'. In fact the papal encyclical *Apostolicae Curae*, which in 1896 condemned Anglican orders as 'absolutely null and utterly void' had to assault the (very slippery) doctrine of 'intention', as the historical case for the continuity of episcopal succession and ordination was impeccable.

(iii) *Orders and priesthood:* here history has played a maverick game with us. Two trends happened simultaneously and then coalesced into one apparently solid position. Trend one was the use of terms of Jewish priesthood about bishops, presbyters, and deacons – a trend well-established by the time of Hippolytus, and even more by the time of Cyprian, in respect of the bishop – he was the 'high priest'. I think I know why (in Cyprian's case he wanted the authority of Aaron, which led in the Book of Numbers to the ground swallowing up the opposition) – but it is a long departure from the teaching of the Epistle to the Hebrews. In time the terms '*hiereus*' and '*sacerdos*' were extended to the presbyters, and the situation was nicely confounded in Anglo-Saxon where the contraction of 'presbyter', i.e. 'priest'. was misleadingly used both to translate into English the Old Testament sacerdotal terminology and also for the parish presbyter. It is a disappointing outcome for us, as the Reformers got their Bible translations accurate and transparent ('*hiereus*' = 'priest': '*presbuteros*' = 'elder'), whilst leaving us with this English-language muddle which contributed strongly to the Oxford Movement's theological effrontery. For myself, I have ceased now to say 'priest' when I mean 'presbyter', and I recommend this simple linguistic change to all. It will help clarify the Church of England's doctrine, and its ecumenical stance, no end.

This trend to sacradotal language coalesced with the second one I said I would be mentioning, a trend by which sacrificial terminology was being used about the eucharist from the early second century onwards. So now, lo and behold, there was a priest with a sacrifice to offer every week in direct contradiction to the Epistle to the Hebrews. The cruder forms of this error of 'eucharistic sacrifice' have been discarded – and the relationship of the role of the individual priest to the structures of the church has had to be re-examined, but here is a question which ought to be openly debated among us (as it was an ARCIC and, up to a point, on the Liturgical Commission). What terminology is needed for the eucharist as well as for the ordained president of it – and what truths are we seeking to protect thereby?

(iv) *Orders and unity:* every time the issue of unity comes up, the cry goes up that it is the clergy and their fussiness about their orders which hinder Christian unity. Sometimes of course the laity are fussed about orders too. And I have a suspicion that it is institutional employment, housing, pensions, and status (particularly for those who enjoy being a one-man band) which inhibit ecumenical progress on the local scene, as much as it is 'orders'. I simply wish to inject a dimension to our ministry which I hope will help those who are ordained in separated denominations. We claim to ordain deacons and presbyters 'in the church of God'. They are called to a visible ministry, which claims to function in a single unbroken catholic church, when in fact the visible church is in a desperately fragmented state. So the calling to ordination should imply not just a harking back to the defensibility of what the Church of

28

England did at the Reformation (though that issue is undoubtedly present at each ordination), but it should also be a daily reminder of the eschatological quest for organic unity which is ours. I do not believe in fragmented orders, which would need infinite numbers of topping up from each other as schisms are healed – but I do believe in the gradual emergence of greater and greater credibility for our claim to be presbyters (not just in the Church of England, but) *in the church of God*, as we make gains, however modest, towards true organic unity. It also means we should endeavour to get ministers of other denominations to think similarly, and we should seek ways by which eschatology as much as past history should then determine how we should view them.

(v) *Orders and headship:* a few brief notes are in order here. It is not at all clear that 'headship' equals 'dominance' – nor, even if it were thought to be so, that the fatherhood role in a family is immediately transferable in the Scriptures to the pattern of the life of the local church. It is a perfectly respectable exposition to understand 'headship' as 'point of origin' (as the spring is the head of the river – and as Adam was 'head' of Eve), and this has then few or no implications of dominance for ongoing relationships. It is also true that in history (as perhaps may also be so in the future) the ministers of the church, who are theoretically servants not masters, have not always actually *had* dominance. I think (as an incongruous example) of those Celtic bishops who were kept concealed in the choirs of monasteries, whilst abbots ran the dioceses. The bishop was simply wheeled out (like a drone on its brief flight) when the church required an ordination. Then he was wheeled back in again. He was a sort of Board of Ministry poodle. I do not commend the model, and personally would have loathed what the episcopal life entailed. But no one could have called it headship. And, at a lowlier level, I am still asking what 'headship', if any, is exercised by a hospital chaplain, or the associate minister of a congregation who takes pastoral charge during a vacancy, or indeed of *any* local presbyter who is under the authority (and 'headship'?) of his or her bishop.

As this bears upon the ordination of women, let me, as a side-issue, offer you a model of the issue the Church of England has been facing. It is as though we were wrestling with a decision to change our traffic rules in order to drive on the right. Traffic has been required to drive on the left for well over 100 years – perhaps even longer than that; its origins lie, as far as I know, lost in the mists of history: in Britain it is an unbroken tradition, conserving and expressing a secure continuity. Indeed it far antedates the motor-car and other modern vehicular inventions – all of which have arisen since and have had to come to terms with it. So the question which will point up the illustrative rule is this: does this unbroken tradition of practice amount to a God-givenness which says that that which has never been changed, can never be changed? You can imagine such a debate entering into channels such as whether this was really a change at all – the underlying principles of order on the roads would be preserved *in toto* – or whether this was the right time for it, of how it affected our international relationship (including, so the alarmists would tell us one, or even two, crossovers from side to side in the Channel Tunnel), how it threatened the British way of life, and even, from some bold spirits, how they would have sorrowfully to continue to drive on the left even when everyone was moving to the right. My point is not to make a cartoon, but solely to point up the kind of reflection needed in respect of the status of an unbroken tradition.

I also want to make a point about sociological conditioning. We might as well acknowledge that society has exercised a leverage upon the church towards women's ordination. But that admission does not settle the issue as to whether the theological case is made out or not. For the argument is even-handed, and we may also observe that in previous centuries it was sociologically impossible for the theological issue to be opened, and that has helped keep things unchanged. A similar theological resistance to the issue is found even today in societies where sociologically women hold a disadvantaged or subservient role.

And I also want to make a point about what it is which

women desire. If you hammer at a door for a long time, you may just possibly not notice how things are changing inside. It would be terrible if women finally achieved ordination as presbyters, but on the basis of an understanding of ordination which derived from the 1960s, and lacked the reforming style and thrust of the 1990s.

I do not suggest these considerations settle the issue of whether women should have 'full' ordination or not. That issue has come to the crunch whilst this book was being prepared for press. But I do suggest that the 'headship' facet should be carefully addressed and unpicked even whilst we proceed to implement the decision, and it *could* (if expounded in one way) have implications for the roles our prospective women presbyters are allowed to take up.

(vi) *Orders and laity* – I repeat what a presbyter said to me a few years ago – that he thought distributing communion was a layperson's role. So it is in our churches today. But until 1970 only a clericalized, screened, specially licensed lay reader in a demonstrably needy parish could administer the elements apart from the clergy – and he only the cup. Similarly thirty years ago no layperson ever read epistle or gospel at communion – let alone led the intercessions. New roles have come in alongside new liturgical rubrics which have permitted much greater freedom. I think the first woman reader was licensed in 1969 – that provision for lay people of either sex to administer either element came in 1970. On the time-scale of history, we are at the very beginning of discovering the role of laity, and their ministry inside and outside the church. I do not confound 'enabling' with 'managing' – and I think we are engaged in 'enabling' – that is we seek to discern what each person's full potential is to be realized in Christ, and we go for that. God forbid we should ever be stunting the growth of laypersons by our love of our own clerical roles.

(vii) *Orders and the Word of God:* I end with not a question, but a sermon. If we revert to our second century models we find the bishop was the place to find the Word of God. The ministerial person and the deposited Word of God were in some marvellous sense continuous with each other. And, of course, the Word is not mere words − it ministers Jesus Christ to us and to others. Ministers are not necessarily to be bothered about waving Bibles around, perhaps − but they are to be indwelt with the Word of God. That is how they begin to minister.

3. The Ministry: Time for reformation

An independent perspective

Peter Cotterell

1. Some Fundamentals

Christianity is perennially in danger of degenerating into mere religion, into superstition, and this is at least in part because the Christian Church is perennially in danger of losing its true focus. The focal concern of Christians ought not to be the continuance and the enlarging of the church. Nor ought it to be the Kingdom of God, for all that the topic of the Kingdom of God is presently the primary pre-occupation of the theologians. The focal concern of Christians, and the focal concern of the Church ought to be God.

Christianity (like Islam and Judaism) recognizes a major distinction, a fundamental distinction, an eternal distinction; that which exists between Creator and created. Christianity also recognizes a unique bridge between these two fundamentally separated categories: God incarnate in Christ. It is Christ who comes amongst us and enables us to know God ('Anyone who has seen me has seen the Father'), and it is Christ who makes it possible for God to know us, not from his remote eternity but from within human flesh ('For we do not have a high priest who is unable to sympathize with our weaknesses, but we have one who has been tempted in every way, just as we are'). Christianity offers a Mediator, one Mediator, between the created, humanity, and the Creator, God. But there is only one Mediator.

This statement is fundamental to any biblical understanding of the Christian ministry: there is only one Mediator. As Paul expressed it: 'For there is one God and one mediator between God and man, the man Christ Jesus, who gave himself as a ransom for all men' (1 Tim 2:5).

This concise statement on the Mediator is required to take a great deal of weight in the following thoughts on the Christian ministry, and so it is right to point out that Paul is deliberately making the unique mediatorial role[1] of Christ analogous to the uniqueness of God. 1 Tim 2.5 is a significantly condensed and unmistakeably fundamental statement: 'One God, One Mediator!' Indeed one writer comments: 'This is one of the most significant verses of the New Testament.'[2]

Thus we may lay the essential foundation for any doctrine of Christian ministry. It must be so phrased, so expressed, as to secure the uniqueness of the one Mediator between God and humanity. However, what we in fact have is the compromising of that unique role given to Christ by the creation of a further fundamental distinction, that between a mediating group, the so-called clergy, and the rest of the church, the so-called laity.

We turn next, and briefly, to the term 'Church'. The significance of this term is confused for us because of its denotations and its connotations. Denotatively the word 'church' relates to a building, and connotatively the word relates to formal church services. The word 'church' in other words, no longer appropriately represents either the Old Testament *qahal* or the New Testament *ekklesia*, each of which denoted a community rather than a congregation. Of course this is not to deny that that community would from time to time meet as a congregation. However the community continued to be a reality, it continued to function as a community, even when it was not a gathered congregation. The first believers could continue functioning as a community when

34

they met other believers in their homes. The *ekklesia* was still the church, even in a home, and functioned as a church even without the presence of the apostles or any other special category of mediator. The people of God were a single community, linked to God through the death and resurrection of Christ, which removed the sin barrier separating them from God, by the Holy Spirit, who interceded with God on their behalf, and by Christ, the one Mediator.

The Christian Church was a community. Within that community people were born, were married, bore children and died. They ate, drank, prayed, worshipped and meditated, enjoyed a *koinonia* sharing, and reached out to the unredeemed world in *philanthropia* (brotherly love). All of these activities were activities of the Christian community. In other words the New Testament concept of the *ekklesia* − community involved a very much larger domain of meaning than the twentieth century concept of the *ekklesia* − congregation. A major reason for this loss of community in favour of congregation is our unreformed doctrine of the Christian ministry.

2. The Christian Ministry

There is an interesting anecdote that is often attached to the Baptist preacher Charles Haddon Spurgeon. He is supposed to have been asked if he was ordained, to which he is said to have replied: 'I cannot see what you putting your empty hands on my empty head would accomplish'. The anecdote has this much to commend it: Spurgeon was not ordained, did not use the title 'Reverend' and remained plain Mr Spurgeon[3] to the end of his life. But whether it was Mr Spurgeon or some other who was responsible for the statement on ordination, he was wrong. The practice of marking the setting apart of an individual for some particular ministry by having someone 'lay hands' on him or her has perfectly good authority both in Old Testament and in New Testament.

However this practice must be distinguished from that which leads to the creation of a priestly class in the Christian community, the clergy. As has frequently been observed, the New Testament is far more concerned with identifying the work to be done in the church than with defining privileged offices within the church.

Indeed the essential one-ness of the Christian community is well illustrated by the frequent use of 'one another' (Gk *allelon*)[4] in the New Testament. We are to pray for one another, to confess to one another, to serve one another, to forgive one another, to teach one another, and all of this without any particular reference to a supposed church hierarchy. And this refusal to divide the community commends itself since it conforms to what Jesus himself had to say on the subject.

In the context of questions concerning the religious hierarchy of the day Jesus specifically forbade the community to adopt distinguishing titles:

> . . . *you are not to be called 'Rabbi', for you have only one Master and you are all brothers. And do not call anyone on earth 'father', for you have one Father, and he is in heaven. Nor are you to be called 'teacher', for you have one Teacher, the Christ. The greatest among you will be your servant. For whoever exalts himself will be humbled, and whoever humbles himself will be exalted* (Mt 23:8–12).

In the light of such a clear and authoritative statement it is surely remarkable that the church took so short a time to introduce such a term as 'Father' for its clergy, and that subsequently we have had so little difficulty in persuading the church to continue the use of distinguishing labels for the clergy, such as 'Reverend'[5]. Jesus quite clearly proposed a community and not a hierarchical congregation. But as Nigel Wright comments:

> *For most of its history, much of the church has chosen to ignore these words completely and do the precise opposite. Jesus intended to form a community in which*

36

*the supremacy of God within it was not to be eclipsed
by the perennial human tendency to seek for status and
position.*[6]

The Christian ministry should be understood as the perception
of the Christian community that its members are variously
gifted, and that for the exercise of these gifts some kind of
formal recognition is appropriate. Understood in this way it
is possible to identify the Christian ministry as being not
monochrome male, nor exclusively connected with preaching,
nor necessarily presidential. The ministry is the people of God,
as a community, recognizing the diverse and sovereign and
inclusive (the opposite of the present exclusive) gifting of the
Holy Spirit, and acting together to facilitate the exercise of the
gifts.

It is not difficult to trace the historic pattern of
development in the Christian concept of the ministry. In the
earliest days of the Church there was recognition of the special
status of the apostles[7]. Gradually structures began to
develop in the nascent Church. No single structure, of course,
but a diverse range of structures, to some extent developed
at the whim of the local Christian community, or perhaps
at the instigation of one of the apostles, or again as prompted
by the Spirit. Those terms which we now attempt to make
conformable to our particular systems of church government
made their appearance: presbyters or elders (*prebyteroi*),
deacons (*diakonoi*), bishops (*episkopoi*), prophets (*prophetai*),
teachers (*didaskaloi*), pastors (*poimenes*), evangelists
(*euangelistai*).

But we search the pages of the New Testament in vain for
any suggestion that among the churches of those days there
was any agreed uniform system of church government. Those
who talk so readily of getting back to New Testament Church
principles seem usually to take to their New Testaments a ready-
made pattern for church government for which they will be
sure to find some measure of biblical authority.

Subsequently various patterns of church government
emerged and were viewed as normative: deacons, elders,

bishops. Just why the teachers and prophets and evangelists were excluded from the hierarchy we do not know. But the distinctions between the three orders of ministry gradually clarified, and what had begun overtly and of set purpose as a servant ministry became a hierarchy, what was expected to be a community became a congregation, with what were meant to be servants turned into masters[8].

The Reformation produced changes, but they were changes of emphasis rather than of essence. The presidential ministry remained. The unbiblical distinction between clergy and laity was not removed.

As it happens this infelicity matters much less than we might suppose. The survival and even the expansion of the Church does not depend on our getting the structures of the church right. It is the genius of the Church that it has no pattern of government that is a guarantee of its health still less of its survival. Like Old Testament Israel the Church survives because of its infinite adaptability[9]. So we have no need to look for some authoritative structure which can guarantee the Church the blessing of God. Wherever two or three gather in the name of Christ there is Christ, and it does not particularly matter what the purpose of that gathering might be. In worship, in prayer, at a meal, in the fields, at work, there is Christ, the one Mediator between humanity and God, the one guarantor of a restored and effective relationship.

However it is not unimportant that the structure of the Church should be conformable to the fundamental principle, that of the priesthood of all believers. The existence of the clergy-laity dichotomy serves to rob the Church of the ministry of many of its ablest people.

And at this point it is reasonable to set down my own understanding of the Christian ministry. It is best expressed in five propositions:

1. *The Holy Spirit* sovereignly gifts each member of the Christian community for the benefit of that community. The Christian ministry is then the sum of all the ministries of those members. Jesus is himself designated our High Priest (Heb 8)

and so the way to God is opened up through him, and no other mediator is necessary.

2. *The concept of a ministry* which divides the Christian community into a laity and a clergy, with the laity in some measure dependent on the priestly intercessions of the clergy, has no support in Scripture. As Howard Snyder expresses it:

> *'The New Testament simply does not speak in terms of two classes of Christians — "ministers" and "laymen" — as we do today. According to the Bible, the people of God comprise all Christians, and all Christians, through the exercise of spiritual gifts, have some "work of ministry" to perform . . . The New Testament doctrine of ministry rests, therefore, not on the clergy/laity distinction, but on the twin and complementary pillars of the priesthood of all believers and the gifts of the Spirit'* (The Community of the King, *IVP, Downers Grove 1977, 94–95. See also the same author's* Liberating the Church, *Marshalls, Basingstoke 1983).*

3. *There is no place* in the Church for the offering of blood sacrifices and insofar as the term 'priest' suggests a related sacrificing role it is inappropriate.

4. *The terms* 'priest' and 'priesthood' as applied to all believers are biblical and appropriate, but these are inclusive terms, not exclusive, and have no reference to the offering of sacrifices or of the re-presentation of Christ's self-offering.

5. *There is*, therefore, no special ministry within the Christian community that is reserved for clergy or priesthood.

In particular we assert that (subject to their being in good standing in the church) all may baptise, all may preside at the communion, all may read the Scriptures in public, all may conduct a funeral service, all may pronounce the absolution.

The Presidential Ministry

In most churches the minister functions in effect as a kind of congregational president. If he is present at all at any of the various meetings of the church, or even of part of the church, he takes the leading role. He chairs the Parochial Church Council or the Church Meeting or the Deacons' Court, or the Court of Elders. And, of course, he takes the lead in those gatherings of the church concerned with worship.

For the immensely varied range of expertise this requires of one man (and the gender problem is very relevant here) a very particular and extended period of training. The Vicar needs to know how to preach, and what is generally (and revealingly) termed priestcraft[10]: how to function as a priest. He must know what to say and what to do and where to stand and even what to wear at all the important points in the church's liturgical cycle[11].

The ministerial training college provides a curriculum and a training programme which is designed to ensure that the ministerial candidate acquires all the needed skills. It is simply not possible to take into account the particular Holy Spirit gifting of the individual, since every minister must be capable of performing the same range of activities. The fact is, of course, that some ministers are good pastors, some are good prophets, some are good teachers and some are good administrators. The college cannot, of course, supply the ministers with the Spirit gifting for this intimidating range of activities, but it can provide the secular equivalent.

A number of consequences follow. First of all ministers have to come to terms with the fact that they are not gifted, nor even capable, in all that is expected of them. Having eventually recognised this (and most eventually do), they have to decide on what action to take. Some work harder at those areas where they are weakest. Others take the diametrically opposite way, and leave undone those tasks for which they have no aptitude. Some have the good sense to look around the church for lay

40

people who can supply the deficiencies. Most soldier on, doing all that is required, to the dismay and gradual disillusionment of their congregations.

A second consequence is that members of the church who have the gifts lacking in the minister may find themselves unwelcome, since their evident ability sets into high relief the comparative ineptitude of the minister.

A third consequence is that the church is robbed of the ministry that would have been developed if only that term had been understood in its inclusive sense, instead of being confused and beclouded by the concept of a presidential ministry. The minister is a poor chairman of committees, but insists on chairing them anyway. The minister is a fine teacher but cares little about worship and music. The minister has a prophetic ministry but is in no sense an evangelist.

Arguably more serious, fourthly, is the consequence for the women of the church. The Bible does teach the submission of the wife to her husband. And this is done not merely on the basis of some appeal to what is seemly, but on the basis of history and theology: 'it was the woman who was deceived . . .' (1 Tim 2:14). And the Bible perceives sex as sacramental, not merely as physical, and takes the relationship between husband and wife as being parallel to that between Christ and Church (Eph 5:23)[12]. The analogy is highly productive, but one consequence is that as it is inconceivable that the Church should take authority over Christ, so it is inappropriate that a wife should take authority over her husband. Thus both the Fall in history and the institution of marriage in sociology make it inappropriate for a woman to become a presidential minister.

Of course theologians will differ in their response to these biblical principles. A dismissive hermeneutic may circumvent the problem entirely: the fundamental authority of the Bible may be rejected. But what cannot be done is to dismiss the notion of the subordination of a wife to her husband as being merely cultural.

A fifth consequence of the presidential model of ministry is the resultant media stereotype:

Viewed from a sociological perspective, the clergyman in Britain today is the object of tenacious stereotypes. At a superficial level these emerge in cartoons and television comedies. Yet at a more profound level every clergyman soon becomes aware of pre-formed public expectations.[13]

It is unwise of the church to ignore that stereotype, or simply to shrug it off as representing a misunderstanding inseparable from lack of spirituality. In fact the stereotype is close to being a caricature. The caricature, the cartoon figure, represents an exaggeration, but it is an exaggeration of something that is there initially to be exaggerated. The caricature should then allow us to see the reality that underlies the exaggeration.

4. Conclusion

When the exaggerations are stripped away it appears that the minister of religion is perceived as an anachronism, an irrelevance in the real world, probably harmless, but not to be taken seriously in any vital issues affecting the community.

It must be stressed that this is a judgement made of the ministry as it now appears in much of the church in the United Kingdom. It is no judgement at all either of the prophetic ministry of the church (which is rarely evident at all) or of the genuine pastoral ministry of the church. The former would be perceived as an irritant, but probably admired nonetheless, the latter would be perceived with wistfulness and admiration, as representing a desperately needed caring element in post-rural society. (Oddly, where the true pastoral ministry continues to operate it is often precisely in rural society, where the traditional caring structures are preserved, rather than in the urban society where they are lost.)

In fact what I would be looking for positively in the future ministry is threefold: an emphasis on a prophetic ministry, a concern for a pastoral ministry and the development of a shared ministry across all existing sections of the church. Negatively I would look to see an end to the division between clergy and laity, and so a rediscovery of the true significance of the priesthood of all believers, an end to the use of clerical titles, and an end to superstition on the one hand, and magic on the other which make the clergy necessary.

What I would not want to see is that alternative error, an egalitarianism which leaves the sheep all equal, but equally unfed and uncared for.

Notes

1. 'One mediator . . . with an implied antithesis, one and not more', Walter Lock in *The Pastoral Epistles* (T. & T. Clark, Edinburgh, 1924, 27).
2. Ralph Earle '1 Timothy' in F.E. Gaebelein (ed), *The Expositor's Bible Commentary* XI, Zondervan, Grand Rapids 1978, 358).
3. A second anecdote also is attached to Spurgeon, that he was asked if he were a Doctor of Divinity. To which he is said to have replied 'I was not aware that the Divinity was in need of a doctor'. It is unfortunate that Spurgeon was (and still is) so casually dismissed as academically negligible. No-one who is familiar with the vast body of Spurgeon's writing, and perhaps most particularly with his magisterial *Treasury of David*, could doubt his profound learning. But still, Mr Spurgeon he remained.
4. See Romans 12:5,10,16; 13:8; 14:13, 19; 15:5,7; and so on, and similarly in Ephesians, 1 John, 1 Peter. J.V. Taylor, comments 'Like a peal of bells the word *allelon* – "one another" – rings through the pages of the New Testament' *The Go Between God* (SCM, London 1977, 126). I am grateful to R.A. Campbell for drawing my attention to Taylor's comment.
5. And there is some fear that the contemporary demand for the ordination of women is linked to the demand by women for the title 'reverend' to be made available to them. It is certainly instructive to note that precisely when the use of such titles and even of clerical dress is in decline among men, women ministers tend to be rather fiercely protective of both. See Robin Gill, *Beyond Decline*, SCM, London, 1948 p. 43, 'It is no accident that clerical dress assumes so important a role for the clergy even when they claim that it does not.'

But if the term reverend is objectionable how much more so, and how absurd, are the further titles, 'Very Reverend' and even 'Most Reverend', and 'Venerable'. Of the latter title as used in the Roman

Catholic Church the dictionary explains 'title of one who has attained a certain degree of sanctity but is not fully beatified' . . .

6. Nigel Wright, *Challenge to Change* (Kingsway, Eastbourne 1991, 117).

7. Although even in the period covering the writing of the New Testament the term 'Apostle' was not applied exclusively to the twelve, nor even to the twelve plus Paul. Others too, including such as Andronicus and Junias could be accorded the title (Romans 16:7).

8. It is ironic that Jesus said of anyone in the church who wished to become great: 'Let him be your minister' (Mt 20:26). We have left his words unchanged but their meaning transformed, 'Let him be your Minister'! Jesus used the word *diakonos*, which was not a hierarchical term for a ruler, but a somewhat demeaning term for a servant.

9. cf T.C. Friezen, *An Outline of Old Testament Theology* (Blackwell, Oxford 1962, 373).

10. See for example, Charles Moore, A.N. Wilson, Gavin Stamp, *The Church in Crisis* (Hodder & Stoughton, London 1976, 91) '. . . the colleges are meant to provide practical training in what the higher establishments call priestcraft'.

11. 'See A.G. Martimort, *The Church at Prayer* (Chapman, London 1985, 99ff) if in doubt about what some scholars see that the priest must know with regard to dress, gesture, prayer, benediction, absolution and so on.

12. Of course any truly biblical marriage begins with the mutual submission of husband and wife, a fact which is concealed by the NIV paragraphing. This provides a paragraph division at the end of verse 21, where the Greek does not even provide a new sentence!

13. Robin Gill, *Beyond Decline* (SCM, London 1988, 43).

4. My personal pilgrimage
A Methodist perspective

Donald English

I was three years of age when I first accepted responsibility in the Methodist Church. My onerous task was to pump the organ. The effectiveness of this ministry was measured by the descent of the lead weight on the side of the instrument. As it came down I was winning; if it went up Mr Huntsman the organist was winning. The competition gave to the services not only an interest but an excitement of a kind rarely matched since.

That early experience of ministry provided me with a vantage point from which to observe worship, and here I received my earliest remembered impressions of the people of God. The chapel (this designation is important) was at one end of a country Circuit in the United Free Methodist Connexion. I have no recollection whatsoever of any ordained minister. Our preachers were laymen. I was baptized by a lay pastor (though I have no conscious memory of that). At the Lord's Supper the bread and wine were distributed by my uncle Will and my uncle George. My mother and auntie ran the Women's Fellowship. My overall impression, as I look back, is of a community accepting total responsibility for its life and witness. If ordained ministry did play a large part in that activity, it was wholly hidden from me.

Our move as a family to another village led to my involvement in an ex-Primitive Methodist church where again the lay leadership was the clue to the life of the church. We then moved again, and another ex-Primitive church deepened this impression. I was fourteen before involvement in a town chapel in the Wesleyan tradition introduced me to regular pastoral care and observable leadership by an ordained minister. After a significant experience of personal commitment to church, however, it was lay leadership of a fellowship class and the Sunday School which contributed most to my Christian growth. At university an inter-denominational group, part of the Inter-Varsity Fellowship, provided the setting for further growth − paralleled by the work of the local Methodist church, where the ordained minister exercised an effective ministry to students.

This rather long biographical introduction serves to underline the fact that for me and perhaps for many young Methodists the ordained minister does not necessarily figure highly in the beginning or the growth of Christian life. And since it is in the setting of the church that the call to ordained ministry often comes, the prospective candidate for the ministry is prompted by the suggestions of lay people, or by a particular friendship with a minister rather than through the normal life of the church itself. In the former case the candidate finds herself or himself moving towards ordained ministry as the 'most obvious' outlet for the gifts and abilities recognized by fellow Christians who offer encouragement in that direction. In the latter case it is often a recognition of quality in the minister(s) who befriends, or a desire to do the things and fulfil the roles which can be *seen* by an observer. In either case, or a combination of the two, certain views of ordained ministry are likely to be uppermost.

The first can be called *charismatic*. A young Christian's growth indicates gifts and abilities within the life of the church, and older Christians observe this. Within his or her own life there is an awareness that such potential is best fulfilled in the context of ministry within or on behalf of the church. The pressing question is whether such gifts and abilities are being used to the full in 'secular', 'lay', employment, with limited voluntary involvement in church life. Are God's gifts being properly used in that setting? If the ordained ministry is seen as the obvious outcome of such a situation, then the resultant (because causative) view of ordination will centre on charismatic insights. The routes into the ordained ministry are likely to be those of vocation and personal fulfilment.

Another view is the *functional* one. The church is looking for people to exercise gifts of leadership. The minister's task is seen along certain lines – preaching, visitation, administration. Those who seem capable of such tasks are likely to be pointed in this direction. Friendship with the minister, in a pastoral setting, will highlight particular tasks. It is not only the task-orientation which is significant here; it is the fact that certain tasks are highlighted. The view of the essential role of the ordained minister thus exercises a strong influence upon the encouragement and selection of recognizable types of candidate. (A Methodist who shows little promise as a preacher is not likely to be encouraged to offer, for example.)

My own experience was of this kind. Questions of ordained ministry were for me largely questions of vocation (what was God calling me to do with my life?); stewardship (how could the gifts God had given be used to the full in his service?); and fulfilment (which parts of my life gave the greatest sense of doing what I was intended to do?). Materials for answering those questions were my daily Bible-reading and prayer, participation in the life of the church, advice from ministers and others about one's suitability, or otherwise, for ordained ministry, reflection upon the logical outcome of one's life, abilities and training so far, and sensitivity to the moments of greatest fulfilment in daily living. In so far as there was any doctrine of ordination involved it was of the functional charismatic kind, since both the church life I knew and the Christian experience I had had raised only that kind of question about ordained ministry. Theologically, Methodist Protestant convictions about the nature of the church and the priesthood of all believers precluded ideas of a separate class of Christians called priests who were ontologically different from the rest.

I therefore went to theological college to train to be a pastor, preacher (one who leads worship and preaches) and administrator. The fact that at that time ministers still largely divided their days to facilitate this threefold task — study in the morning, visiting in the afternoon, meetings in the evening — encouraged such a picture. College training did, of course, raise the question of ordination, but a functional charismatic view was defensible, fitted well into Methodist Deed of Union Statements, and accorded with what I observed in the lives of ministers I knew.

On reflection I can see, though I wasn't very much aware of it at the time, that the first question mark against this as a total view of ordination was raised by a decision of the church about my own future. Instead of leaving college to be the pastor/preacher/administrator I wished to be, I was appointed to teach in theological college. After two years of that I was ordained, having been a probationer, passed the necessary examinations and received the appropriate commendations. But I had not functioned in the role I had envisaged, nor would I after ordination, for I was on my way to a theological lectureship overseas. The charismatic element could survive scrutiny. Since I was able and trained as a teacher it would be logical to teach (though why I *needed* to be ordained to do so was not so clear). The functional view was less intact. The trouble was that, by and large, I wasn't functioning in Methodism in the manner understood by that view. (The fact that connexional secretaries and other tutors weren't doing so either was in no sense a solution.)

My ordination took place, nevertheless, and I understood it largely in terms of God (both personally and through the church) confirming his call to me and giving me (personally and through the church) the authority to be a minister in the church. From my side it was a re-affirmation of my response to that call, a promise to accept the discipline of God through the church (including appointment to teach the New Testament in Nigeria) and a renewed commitment to God's service. I believed he was giving and would give me the grace I needed. It was therefore a point in a process; a significant culmination of some things and beginning of others. It expressed liturgically and symbolically what I believed to be true and what the church

48

by its action was affirming to be true. Within the boundaries of God's call, the church's confirmation, my response and training, there was a status conferred, a discipline imposed, a promise of strength for the task, and the knowledge of an appointment to be filled. As such the ordination was significant, appropriate and important, though it lacked for me the high emotional tone of the experience of a fellow ordinand who used electrical terms to describe his feelings as hands were laid on him and the words spoken.

Years in theological teaching overseas provided two new influences related to this subject. One was the importance of *status* in African culture. It was not only important, it had to be reflected in dress, station, style of life and protocol. Although the Westerner might be forgiven for feeling that questions of worthiness and efficiency also enter in, there is an obvious security for all involved, and a strong sense of one's place in any situation, when status, rank and honour are given high priority.

The other influence was exerted by representatives of other denominations with whom I worked closely. The acceptance of episcopacy, for example, and the sense of priesthood even among evangelical Anglicans, which differed from most Methodist ideas of ministry, provided new perspectives on one's own views. Pressures for church union were as influential in Nigeria as in England during the same period of time. One had to ask why some fellow-Christians saw things in a different light. Yet one was also committed to defending what one believed to be a true doctrine of ministry against other views which were either contrary to biblical teaching or gave the impression that only one understanding of ministry was defensible on biblical and other grounds.

There were two separate problems here. One was the pressure to seek union with all other Christians. The other was how far one could go in accepting a differing view of ministry from one's own as definitive, or how far one should resist such views in the interests of truth. Within a vortex of this kind all one's opinions undergo severe testing. The study of statements of belief, of draft ordinals, of the welter of books, pamphlets and papers which surround both the long discussions with fellow-Christians of a variety of viewpoints, and the self-examination of one's own position, convictions and loyalties, bring cherished ideas and attitudes under fresh scrutiny.

It is easy, from this vantage point, to give over-clear definitions to insights and convictions which emerged during that period of time in the 1960s and early 70s. But for the sake of clarity some such attempt must be made.

First, one came to see that questions of *order in the church* required a higher place in relation to *the faith of the church* than I had previously allowed. It is easy, raised in what is after all a denomination founded on revival and a deep personal experience, to view formal and institutional discipline as largely unnecessary if only everyone involved would walk with the Lord and obey the Spirit. Instances of 'hierarchical' heavyhandedness, and of 'bureaucrats' who are alleged to lack spiritual vigour and insight, encourage such attitudes.)

Judgements of this kind may sound strange coming from a Methodist, recalling the discipline exercised among the earliest of John Wesley's followers. It is important to recall, however, that his discipline was largely a matter of personal discipline exercised by him alone − even in the setting of the early conferences. He was to them a father, not an ecclesiastical dignitary. His authority was based on his own worth, vision, ability and character; not on institutional status. The latter kind of authority arose in Methodism after his death, and the first half of the nineteenth century tells the sad story of divisions and separations as a result (though institutional authority was not the only cause of unrest during those years). Nevertheless, just as the Methodist way to improve worship is not traditionally to alter the liturgy but to call the congregation to examine its heart before God, so there is a tendency in Methodism to view with suspicion all hierarchical and institutional figures − save perhaps one, the President, whom it has chosen, who lasts for one year only, and whose power obviously attaches to the office rather than to the person.

During the hectic years of union debate in Nigeria, then, after my return, in England, I came to attach greater significance to order than hitherto; and to formal structures for achieving and preserving order. Within such structures the question of office and status naturally arises, and I learned at that time to face the fact that in the New Testament Church status *did* matter, and that St Paul himself was not averse to calling for obedience because of the status of apostle which he claimed for himself. This was not a new discovery for me, of course, but it received a 'higher rating' in my categories of thought about ministry than hitherto. Thus episcopacy expressed through an episcopate (historic or otherwise) did not of itself hold for me a threat, by contrast with our Methodist leadership titles of President, Chairman and Superintendent, which all carry functional rather than status connotations, both by their exercise and by their impermanence.

It was within this setting that I was able to see the ordained minister in more than a functional and charismatic light. Another possible perspective saw him as having a status within an ordered system of church life, *representing* divine authority and church authority within the church and to the world outside the church.

On the other side, however, certain balancing convictions were hardened, and some of them are inextricably linked.

I found myself rejecting more strongly than ever the idea that any one structure of ministry – the threefold order of bishop, priest, deacon was a case in point – could be shown to be unquestionably required by biblical teaching for the life of the modern church, even if it could be shown to be universally accepted and practised in the New Testament Church, which I doubt. One could only judge that if this was the form of ministry which the New Testament writers wished to record and advocate as of universal application to the life of the church in their time and ours then they did a bad job. Nor were the claims being made for this particular form of ministry, in particular the historic episcopate, self-evidently true. The attempt therefore, as a matter of divine purpose, to impose such a form of ministry upon all the churches was both improper (in my judgement) and was based, as I heard Professor C. K. Barrett say some years ago, on bad theology and bad history. It is bad theology because the biblical basis for it is inadequate. It is bad history because there is too little evidence for its failure to achieve precisely what it alone is said to preserve in the life and witness of the church.

That there were biblical principles of Christian ministry which were and are essential to the life of the church was something of which I became increasingly certain. That particular offices or structures invariably had preserved or were intended to preserve such principles in every place at every age of the church I doubted, and doubt very strongly.

Perhaps more basically still I came during those years of union negotiations to mistrust an emphasis which involved safeguarding the ordained ministry as a way of safeguarding the life of the church. Too much of the union material was concerned exclusively with questions of ordained ministry. Of course it can be argued that these were the major centres of controversy between the denominations, but this reply merely pushes the question one step further back. Why *must* it be the case that when sacraments are discussed the debate inevitably and unerringly moves on to questions of ordained ministry? They are not, after all, the preserve of the ordained. Or have they become so? And if so, is this healthy? Why was it that at every stage the dialogue about major elements in the life of the church – worship, initiation, sacraments, preaching, discipline, legislation – turned into disagreements about ordained ministry? It seemed increasingly clear to me that this was the result of the error of 'defining the church by its clergy'; of making the 'ordained ministry' the focal point and essential element in the life of the church. To the argument that these issues dominate our union discussions because they are precisely the points of difference one can only reply that the debate should be about the presuppositions and developments which have caused them to be the markers of divergence instead of the rallying points of reconciliation. The indications seemed to be that the ordained ministry had become altogether too exclusive, powerful and normative within the life of the church. In so becoming it had often stifled the spiritual growth and effectiveness of the nonordained Christian family.

Such convictions were strengthened for me by my experience of circuit ministry (at last), and my theological reflections after returning to theological college work (again). Other convictions, however, grew up alongside them during those years.

In circuit I served a large and flourishing suburban church and a small and struggling church on a council estate. In both situations I found myself becoming clearer on two separate issues. One concerned the context of evaluating the meaning of ordained ministry. The other concerned the nature of the ordained minister's task.

As far as context was concerned, it was increasingly borne in upon me in circuit that the ministry of the whole church was the major setting in which to consider ordained ministry. This was not the first time such thoughts had occurred to me, but they were now reinforced unmistakably by my life in circuit. My particular stations surrounded me with many devout, able and active lay Christians. The life of both churches was warm, spiritual and issued in service to each neighbourhood. My ministry was meaningful as it overlapped and complemented that of my lay brothers and sisters. My ministry as an ordained person did not give theirs its authority or validity any more than theirs did mine. Both − all − types of ministry, lay and ordained, were authorized and validated by God, and in such a setting it became possible properly to view the Body of Christ in that place, and properly to assess the meaning of one's ordained ministry.

Understanding one's ordained ministry as part of the total ministry of the church, and not as superior or inferior to any other part, had a number of significant results. One was, for example, being free to be ministered to, by lay people, as well as to minister to them. In meetings with church stewards I experienced very deep fellowship and received, as well as exercised, ministry. Such a view also facilitated and helped to create a sense of teamwork in the life of the church. Hierarchical structures, with the ordained minister at the apex of the triangle, were not the framework within which we operated. Individuals and committees were free to get on with their work without my authorization, supervision or checking.

It was, after all, as much their church as mine (in fact it is God's!), and when I had moved on many of them would still be there. God's call, not my presence, validated their work. And I was free to make mistakes. The minister need not be viewed as the best Christian around, any more than he ought to be viewed as omnicompetent. Mine was not a superior ministry, but a different one.

The greatest difficulty arising from such a method of assessing ordained ministry is, of course, to identify where precisely the difference lies between this and lay ministry. It is difficult simply to isolate one activity or another in a purely functional way. Preaching, visiting, administration counselling, teaching are all done by lay people, some of whom are better at it than some ministers. Lay people baptize, though exceptionally rather than as a rule. Ministers marry and make members, though in the latter case for Methodists the significant moment is not the service of confirmation but the vote of the Church Council, almost all of whom are lay, that the persons should be members. The minister presides at the Lord's Supper, yet lay people are increasingly sharing parts of that ministry, and some lay people are given authorization by the Methodist Conference to preside in exceptional circumstances. It is not easy to establish the difference on a functional basis alone. There are few things an ordained minister does which no lay Christians do. He does not necessarily do all these things more than lay Christians do. Some retired lay Christians *may* do more visiting; some professionally or voluntarily may do more counselling; some undoubtedly do more church administration. It is difficult not to see how any lay person could do more preaching than the average circuit minister, but in other denominations it might just be possible. The one major functional distinction is that while most of the minister's tasks are performed by one lay person or another, generally only he does them all, and is authorized and expected to do them all. (The expectation is not so great where ministers are appointed to administrative or teaching posts, but they are exceptions.)

Similar problems exist in connection with the charismatic

view of ordained ministry. That certain gifts are required for such a calling is generally accepted. It is likely, therefore, that ordained ministers will differ from *some* lay people in possessing such gifts. But who would argue that *all* Christians who *are* so gifted *will* be called into ordained ministry? And who would be courageous (or foolhardy) enough to draw up a list of minimum gifts required as essential qualifications for ordained ministry? And to what extent or in which balance are these gifts to be possessed and exercised? This way of establishing the difference between ordained and lay simply will not do. Apart from being unworkable as a criterion it comes dangerously close to limiting God's sovereignty in calling men and women into ordained ministry.

This kind of argument does not dispense with functional and charismatic views of ministry as important ways of viewing ordination. Nor are they wholly irrelevant to the question of boundaries between lay and ordained. But they cannot stand alone in establishing such boundaries.

It is at this point that one returns to the idea of the minister as a *representative person*. Such a view does not exclude functional and charismatic approaches. In fact it needs them. They provide a context of work done and persons gifted to do it. They also safeguard representative ordination against becoming something purely private and inward rather than something evidenced in life and work.

The exact nature of this representative element needs defining with great care, however. After all, every Christian 'represents' the Christian church and the Christian gospel. People expect a Christian to know and believe what Christians believe, to live as Christians lived, to go to church as Christians do, and to adopt the attitudes which Christians adopt – though all within broad limits. What is more, they judge the church by the Christians. In this sense we cannot avoid being representatives – all of us.

Yet some lay Christians are viewed as 'more representative than others'. An office holder, for example, is viewed as more representative of the church, or as representative in a different way, by both Christians and non-Christians. He exercises leadership within the church and is therefore expected to know more about its life. Christians of his persuasion will take a lead from him, ask advice of him, perhaps even model themselves upon him. They are not limited to leaders for any such help, of course, but there is an appropriateness and an expectation where leaders are concerned because, by reason of appointment, ability and status, they are representatives. In that sense they sum up, in themselves, by position and function, what is in fact true of all the church.

People outside the church make a distinction between the representative nature of lay leaders and the function of all Christians in representing Christianity. Yet leadership representation differs in degree rather than kind from the rest, and it is not exclusive.

A similar case can be made out for the representative nature of ordained ministry. Christians and non-Christians expect a level of representation by reason of the status of the ordained minister. Moreover, the nature of his representative status is different. The ordained minister has sensed a 'call' from God. has submitted to scrutiny and selection, training and testing, discipline and duty in a system leading to ordination. This system, in its combined parts and as a whole, is different from all other processes within the church. The nature of the minister's commitment is different, too, in terms of the discipline accepted and the role adopted. In all of these senses he is a representative of the church in a way which lay people are not. Moreover, the ordained minister gathers up all the representative functions in himself or herself though not in the sense that others do not perform them.

The major question is whether this representation is different in degree or kind from that of the lay Christian. Could the line not just as easily be drawn between Christians who do not hold office and those who do (including lay and ordained)? Or should this kind of line be drawn anyway? Putting it more traditionally, is ordained ministry Christ's gift to the church, in a particular sense, or is it one of many gifts to the church, including all that lay people do within its life? Is it Christ's gift to the church, or one of his many gifts *from within* it?

Can it — or ought it — in any sense to be viewed apart from the church, or always and only within it?

The Methodist Church seems to me to come down clearly on the second of these ways of expressing the matter, saying of its ordained ministers that 'they hold no priesthood differing in kind from that which is common to all the Lord's people and they have no exclusive title to the preaching of the gospel or the care of souls. These ministries are shared with them by others to whom also the Spirit divides His gifts severally as He wills.' A little later the Deed of Union adds 'The Methodist Church holds the doctrine of the priesthood of all believers and consequently believes that no priesthood exists which belongs exclusively to a particular order or class of men but in the exercise of its corporate life and worship special qualifications for the discharge of special duties are required and thus the principle of representative selection is recognised.' In these statements the charismatic, functional and representative elements are all clearly to be observed. This does not mean that the ordained minister is solely, or even primarily, answerable to an institution. 'Christ's Ministers in the Church are Stewards in the household of God and Shepherds of His flock.' They are Christ's ministers, and as such are stewards and shepherds, answerable to God, whose household and flock they care for. Yet all others who 'minister' in the Church are equally called and answerable.

The way in which a balance can be achieved in practice within the Church is indicated by examination of another way of assessing ordained ministry, so far alluded to, but not specifically outlined. This is the *vocational* element. The Methodist Deed of Union stresses this way of viewing ordained ministry. 'It is the universal conviction of the Methodist people that the office of the Christian Ministry depends upon the call of God . . .' Yet the individual's sense of and claim to such a call is not of itself sufficient ground for being ordained. Thus God 'bestows the gifts of the Spirit, the grace and the fruit which indicate those whom He has chosen'. Those who are ordained 'by the imposition of hands' are those 'whom the Methodist Church recognises as called of God'.

In this way the preeminence of God's call is preserved. But the individual's sense of call is tested by the church and in the light of God's gifts of grace and fruit of the Spirit for the fulfilment of the task. It may be that it is around this centre that some kind of consensus about ordained ministry might emerge.

Arising from such a consideration, though not wholly dependent upon it, is the question of authority. For the ordained minister it has at least two separate parts. One is the nature of his authority *within* the Church; the other is the nature of his authority, as a minister, in the world *outside* the Church. In particular those engaged in forms of service and caring.

Within the church the model of authority has for centuries reflected attitudes to authority in the community at large. Pyramidal structures have been upheld and used in government, business, armed forces and families for centuries. At the apex of the triangle stands − or perhaps more appropriately, sits − the figure with greatest authority, be he prime minister, managing director, general or father. When such an authority structure is applied to the church, the apex figure is the minister or priest. Such authority is confirmed by the tendency to view him as a professional Christian, leading amateurs whose professional status is enjoyed at work but not in the church. If the minister leads all or most of the services and chairs all or most of the meetings then the pyramid shape of ecclesiastical authority in the local church is still further reinforced.

Each of the views of ordination adumbrated so far in this chapter can be advanced to support such an authority structure. In functional terms 'it is his job'. On a charismatic interpretation 'he does it so well'. From the representative point of view 'it is his rightful position'. It is not surprising that such a system has operated fairly widely in all the churches for a long time − and often with commendable success.

Three considerations, however, provide grounds for unease about such a situation. The first and most obvious is the changed attitude towards authority in our culture at the present time. If being bracketed with the squire and the schoolmaster

58

as the third bastion of authority used to be a source of strength to the minister, it is rarely so these days. In our modern society authority is not so much conferred as earned. Readiness by one person to assume authority has always required willingness on the part of others to recognize and accept its exercise over them. This is not new. But previously it was seen as appropriate for the squire, the schoolmaster and the minister to claim authority. Therefore people were willing to submit to its exercise over them by such professions. This is now much less the case. The ordained ministry has suffered from the steady erosion of 'statutory' authority (alongside most other professions).

At this point the functional and representative views of ordination are likely to be less helpful than the charismatic. As authority is detached from status the minister's right to function as head of every activity will be (and is currently) called in question. The functional approach is thus seen to be a plank of the very platform which is being dismantled.

Nor is the representative perspective much more successful. To claim authority because one represents the wider body within the church is easily turned into a defence of the pyramid which is no longer accepted. Why should the ordained minister be the authoritative person who represents the church at large in every aspect of the life of the local church? Does ordination automatically establish the minister at this apex point in every sphere? If it is so viewed, then why is it? If it is not, then why are so many ministers expected to operate as though it were?

It is the charismatic approach which is most likely to prevail in an atmosphere where authority has to be earned rather than assumed. It may be the general quality of the minister's life, it may be the exercise of particular gifts, it may be the visionary and prophetic nature of his or her leadership, which inspires people to acknowledge and accept the minister's authority. Where these qualities are lacking it is much less likely that they will do so in the modern climate of opinion.

For many modern Christians this development will be a welcome one. A charismatic view of ordination brings with it a charismatic view of lay Christianity too. Alongside the

59

ordained minister's gifts one must place the gifts of the lay members of the church. If the minister is not regarded as having authority in a given area of the life of the church, because of not being gifted in that area, it is likely that some of the lay people will be so gifted and will be seen as possessing and exercising authority at that point. The church is thus seen to operate as a body, each playing his or her part – both ordained and lay – and each exercising whatever authority goes with the gift exercised. The one head of such a body is Jesus Christ and there is no one intermediary.

Such a picture is not as complete as it seems, however, nor a total solution to the problem either. Can an ordained minister's authority ever be gauged by the extent of gifts and the effectiveness of exercise of them? Is authority in any institution capable of being measured in this quantitative way? And even if it were, by whom would it be so measured? Who determines the extent or effectiveness of an ordained minister's gifts and allocates authority accordingly? Then there is the important consideration that God has given to his church not only *ordained ministers* but also *ordained ministry*. Each minister represents not only his or her own life and work but also a wider entity of which the minister is only a part. It must be seriously doubted whether the charismatic view, with its particularist and individualistic tendencies, provides adequately for a holistic view of ordained ministry, though it understandably does in its view of the local church, with the ordained ministry operating alongside all other ministries.

A second major source of unease about pyramidal structures of authority with the ordained minister at the apex is the way in which such a pattern masks the servant nature of the ministry. After all, 'minister' does mean 'servant'. And although an ordained minister may have a sense of being primarily *God's* servant, we do think and speak of 'ministering' to *people*. 'Your servant for Christ's sake' was St. Paul's way of expressing it. However the minister may feel about it, a minister sitting at the top of a hierarchical authority structure will experience a disturbing conflict of roles and attitudes.

Here the functional view of ordination may prove least

helpful. Structures can determine function. Charismatic insight may or may not clarify the situation, depending upon the gifts of the minister. The representative view is most likely to ensure some tolerable resolution of inevitable tension. Authority in leadership and meetings, in services and teaching, does not need to rely upon a structure with a certain shape. It can be seen as depending upon a certain person, after appropriate selection, training and testing, being recognized as holding authority as a representative of the Church, and of Jesus Christ in the church. Such a person need not be at the top of every ladder, nor in the chair at every meeting, nor in the seat of honour at every function. Authority does not rest in such a system, nor need such bolstering up for its exercise. Neither does it hinder a 'servant ministry' nor feel threatened by one. This combination of authority and service, so clearly seen in Jesus Christ, is a crucial element in all the ordained ministry.

The third origin of unease about authority depending upon hierarchy is the nature of grace. In biblical teaching grace is essentially an offer not a command. It is also vulnerable rather than protected. The death of Jesus Christ on the Cross is the supreme example of this. If the ordained ministers are to be representatives of such grace they themselves must demonstrate its characteristics. At this point it is none of the three views outlined − functional, charismatic and representative − which provides the clue. It is *the nature of the call* to ordained ministry. Such a call comes to those who have already experienced God's grace in Christ, or how else could they or why else would they be called? And the call itself comes *as* grace. It is an offer of a part of the Lord's purposes for his church in the world. As such it is vulnerable. It can be ignored, neglected or rejected. It is true that to ignore, neglect or reject grace is to diminish oneself, but the essential vulnerability of grace is not removed by that aspect of reality and experience. What is more, the person who responds to the call must live by grace. The minister not only proclaims good news of God's grace: he or she lives on the strength of such good news. The exercise of authority must be all of a piece with the message proclaimed and the life-style followed.

Authority which grows out of grace is a risky business. For it offers, rather than imposes itself. It is essentially vulnerable. It has no props to lean upon. Its availability, its exercise and its acceptance by others all operate within the area of grace and on the basis of its presuppositions. A minister who exercises authority in this way will be constantly driven back to Christ as his pattern and the Lord as his strength.

The picture of ordained ministry which emerges thus far is a varied and many-sided one. It does not depend on one view but on several. Each will provide its own perspectives and dimensions. They will in turn be more or less important, depending upon the circumstances and their requirements. But all are required for a whole picture, and each will find its source and pattern in Jesus Christ himself.

I end by noting three developments in the exercise of ordained ministry. One I regret, the other two I commend though I discern not enough evidence of them in the church today.

The development I *regret* is what I would call a 'ministry of the gaps'. It operates only in those areas of life which are as yet untouched or uncontrolled by the growing influence of social and health care. Wherever official help is not available, such ministry is present. Thus the minister squeezes into the steadily decreasing space allowed for him by the psychiatrist, doctor, social worker and others of the 'caring' and 'serving' professions. Such space is not only decreasing, it is becoming distinctly cramped. A corollary of this situation is the number who leave neighbourhood ministry to join the professions listed above in order to have a 'man-size' job. (Of course not all who make such a move do so for this reason, and still fewer would express it in this way.)

That ministers should operate in the areas untouched by provisions of the welfare state is not in doubt. But that such should be the *limit* of such ministry must be strongly denied. Such a situation is not only a diminution of ministry. It diminishes Christian theology and ultimately one's vision of God.

In practical terms ordained ministry is required not only to visit the sick in hospital and home but also to have a theological understanding of persons, health and human responsibility which enables comment upon the entire system of health care in our country. We need not only a proper exercise of charity to those in need but also discernment of those injustices in theory, relationships and structures which give rise to the needs. And we require a passion for justice and righteousness which spills out beyond the areas of 'churchly activity' into the whole area of life around us. Most of all we need a theological understanding of humanity and its environment in relation to God which enables others to see that there is more to human nature and needs than can be supplied by social and welfare agencies. From this point of view theology is not simply one academic discipline alongside many others, taking its chance with the rest. It is the understanding of God which sheds light upon all other disciplines; that response to God which provides perspective on all life's relationships, that perception of reality which puts one in touch with the meaning of existence. Ministry based upon such understanding can never be limited to other people's gaps. Its purview is all of life, lived by all people in all places.

The first development I *look* for concerns the minister as theologian. There is in most denominations a fairly well-set pattern of expectation where the work of the ordained minister is under discussion. It includes pastor, preacher, administrator, person of prayer, and a variety of other things. Different traditions have different emphases, but in the main a fairly common picture emerges. Congregations, by their expectations, exert considerable influence upon their ministers to conform to the pattern. Few seem to expect the minister to be a theologian.

Part of the reason for this lack of expectation may be the associations of theology for many Christians. It represents for them an academic, difficult, esoteric discipline, pursued by the highly educated, often to the detriment of Christian faith and assurance. Such Christians find theological books difficult to read, theological fashions as transitory as any other, and theological preachers boring and unintelligible. Their cry is for simpler preaching and teaching, easier to understand and more related to everyday life.

At the level of academic theology many such criticisms would be valid in the setting of worship and Christian instruction. The professional, academic theologian is not concerned about the influence of the latest theory upon the congregations up and down the country. The theologian's task is to use the resources at his or her disposal to push back the barriers of ignorance as far as possible in as disinterested a manner as possible.

Yet the faith of the people of God is important. Their experience of him in everyday life, their search for truth within their experience, their knowledge gained by a variety of activities is also significant for theology.

My plea for ministers as theologians is probably therefore a plea for ministers as theological interpreters. The gap between the academic theologian and the church member is already too wide and seems to be growing. We need generations of ministers who can understand both and be agents of communication across the gap. Otherwise we stand in grave danger of academic theology losing its essential link with the exercise of faith: while the faith of the Church may lose its vital core of intellectual fibre and vigour. To stand between the two, not as umpire but as living link, is no easy task. The ordained ministers are not the only ones who can exercise such a ministry, but they above all are required to do so.

In order to fulfil this function their grasp of both sides of the divide will need to be strong. There will be the necessity to discover again and again the truth that the most lasting theology is done on one's knees. It is an exercise in 'exploring with awe', but there will also be the requirement to worship with one's mind; using all one's intellectual powers to grasp even the fringes of God's being. And there is the task of seeing divine reality in its relationship to daily life. To stand with one foot in the Bible and one in the twentieth-century world and to take the strain by standing on both feet is not an easy calling. Yet God's people need help to do so, and it is part of the service rendered by the ordained ministry – perhaps the major service, for it permeates every part of the minister's task as it is more popularly viewed. As pastor, preacher, administrator, person of prayer, the minister will need deep theological insight if the ministry is to be grounded in God and in the realities of daily living.

The other development I look for is also in the nature of a bridge operation. But this will operate differently. I refer to the bridge across the gap between what happens in the life of the church and what takes place daily in the life of its members in the world. Emphasis upon the minister as the person at the centre of the community of faith (and the word 'parson' is directly linked to the word 'person' – *the* parson is *the* person) so easily results in the ordained minister being virtually locked up within the activities of the church. When that becomes the case the loyalty to the minister, and all that the minister stands for, leads increasingly to lay Christians also being locked up within the activities of the church – usually on church premises. Thus, bit by bit, the club mentality of the church is re-inforced, to the increasing exclusion of all others.

I look – and plead – for a greater sense that the minister is meant to operate not only as the centre of the church but also as its circumference, indeed in all those places where church and world have inter-face. The minister is not meant to 'do' the mission of the whole church in the world, far from it. But the minister ought constantly to be pointing and equipping the church for that mission, and often leading it out there. If that means spending less time within the life of the church, and particularly its organisational structures, then that is a price well worth paying. In a Decade of Evangelism we need all our ministers to be constantly pointing to the nature and necessity of the missionary task. It is this missionary task which has priority in determining the shape of the church, and the ministry is no exception to that.

5. Robes or overalls?

A 'New Church' perspective

Roger Forster

Introduction

Our understanding of the nature and calling of the church of Christ determines our definition and practice of Christian ordination. Therefore, a denomination's perception of itself as a church will govern what it thinks of ordination, how it is exercised and conferred. As we examine the concept of ordination, the fundamental and first question is, 'Is the community of believers an institutional or an inspirational body?' Or in other terms, 'Is the church traditional or charismatic?' Neither term should be understood by popular, current, limited definitions, but rather more generally. Is the church's primary function to preserve and pass on the faith 'entrusted to the saints' (Jude 3), or is its function to receive directly from and be enlightened by God's Spirit of wisdom and revelation (Eph 1.17−22)? Is Christianity a 'monument to the past' or a 'movement into the future'? Does it wear robes or overalls?

It would be too simplistic to respond to these questions with the answer that both alternatives are true. The questions help to determine the primary purpose of the church and therefore to identify what are the essential things which must be unhindered in the church's practice. In church history it is often lesser issues that seem to predominate and lesser goals that take precedence, preventing the fulfilment of the church's pre-eminent calling.

So we must ask another question, 'What do the Scriptures say?' In other words, what kind of community did Jesus set up and intend to continue? In the final analysis it is this kind of church alone which is valid, although God, in his indulgence of us and his long-suffering, puts up with our aberrations, waywardness and ignorance throughout the centuries. His accommodation to our alternative definitions and reinterpretations of his purposes, even if they are hallowed by centuries of mis-practice, should not blind or paralyse us, and keep us from energetic rediscoveries of his mind. 'There is more light to break forth from God's Word', said John Robinson at the departure of the Mayflower.

What, then, essentially distinguishes these two understandings of the 'people of God', and what difference does this make to our view of ordination?

Definitions

Some dictionary definitions of ordination are: (1) 'The arrangement into ranks or classification'; (2) 'The conferring of holy orders admitting to church ministry'; (3) 'decreeing'. These are the commonly understood meanings of the word, but they hold their own problems for many believers. For example, (1) 'arrangement into ranks or classification' might be an acceptable definition to an institutional church and indeed may be regarded as essential, but could be misunderstood and highly offensive to those who believe that the greatest rank in the church is to be servant of all: 'Also a dispute arose among them as to which of them was considered to be greatest. Jesus said to them, "The kings of the Gentiles lord it over them; and those who exercise authority over them call themselves benefactors. But you are not to be like that. Instead, the greatest among you should be like the youngest and the one who rules like the one who serves. For who is greater, the one who is at the table or the one who serves? Is it not the one who is at the table? But I am among you as one who serves'' ' (Lk 22.24–27) Jesus' words here seem to challenge this definition.

(2) 'The conferring of holy orders admitting to church ministry' would also be questioned by an inspirational church which insists that God alone *confers* and the church *recognizes* the endowment: 'Paul, an apostle – sent not from men nor by man, but by Jesus Christ and God the Father, who raised him from the dead' (Gal 1.1).

As for (3) 'decreeing', a perhaps trivializing response to this definition would be, 'It is God who decrees. Who worries what man, or even the church, determines?'

Such definitions are inadequate and in the strongly institutional understanding of them they seem inappropriate to many believers. Even so, some would argue that an institutional view of ordination with its robes or special dress is essential to the church.

Robes or Overalls?

Robes are the public designation and declaration of an office. The function of an office is to preserve and perpetuate the tradition and wisdom of the past and pass them on to the coming generations, thereby providing a kind of social glue, a way of preserving the solidarity of a community of people. The constitution of royalty, of government, of legislative and educational bodies each contains these elements of continuity for the well-being of society. The mayor's chain of office, Mr Speaker's quaint dress in the House of Commons, the wig of a judge, the mortar boards and gowns of academics, the ceremonial dress of the military and knights of the Realm are there to express and play their part in the 'offices' of institutions necessary to hold a people together in a common history, common values, understanding and loyalty. Surely the church, it might be argued, has a similar role to play? It passes on the truths of history and creates a unity and a continuity by its institutions, traditions and testimony to past victories in moral and spiritual realms. Therefore, like royalty and the rest the church should be seen in its official garments which emphasize its office and not its personalities. So then, ordinations are important in placing officials into positions for continuing service into society. This argument is persuasive, logical and attractive. The only problem for some Christians is that, while recognizing the cogency of this view and the benefits of such an institution to society the question remains: is this the kind of church that Jesus founded and was this the purpose for which he brought it into existence?

Unity in Apostolic Succession or Holy Spirit Procession?

If the argument for the importance of structural office to the continuity and unity of the church through the centuries is correct this would naturally be expressed in its valid ordination of persons into ministerial offices so that the function of those offices can continue. This concept no doubt lies behind the idea of apostolic succession and its current outworking recommended by the World Council of Churches statement *Baptism, Eucharist and Ministry* (WCC, Geneva 1982, 22). It is there maintained that the recognition of the three-fold ministry of bishop, presbyter and deacon may serve today as an 'expression of the unity we seek and the means of achieving it'. Further appealing to history, it then goes on to exhort churches without this three-fold ministry to ask themselves whether this pattern does not have a powerful claim to be accepted by them. This suggests that the authors of *Baptism, Eucharist and Ministry* believe that the unity of the church is to be found in its structures; not in the living body, but in the clothes; not in its building together, but in its scaffolding.

However, for some of us the existence and continuance of the church does not reside in its three-fold ministry. We do not think that by accommodating the three-fold ministry and accepting it as the basis of the unity of the church, we would retain its apostolic nature. Rather we judge that, instead of preserving unity, this type of structure creates a false unity, one we cannot find in Scripture and consequently one which continues to stimulate division.

The continuance of the church and its unity resides in the Holy Spirit (Eph 4.3; Jn 14.6), who is, of course, a gift from God, and so also is the unity he brings with him, which we must hold onto and keep. This unity is the heart of Jesus and the fruit of the cross where all our divisions and differences were crucified. Through the cross unity and reconciliation were given to us as a gift from God, not as a goal for the church to try to attain by manipulating people and structures.

If the Holy Spirit is the continuing unity of the church, his activity will be expressed in inspirational and charismatic movements which adhere to the apostolic doctrine (Acts 2.42) since this is also Spirit-breathed (2 Tim 3.14–17). It is not the 'apostolic succession' in its commonly understood form which ensures unity but the Holy Spirit's 'procession' through the centuries maintaining the Spirit-inspired truths of Scripture, which sadly the 'apostolic succession' has often failed to do, despite its claim to represent and preserve the Christian faith.

'The Ordination of the Nail Pierced Hands'

Those of us coming from churches which we believe have been brought into being by the Holy Spirit himself, but which may seem to lack a formal historical tradition (although we would aver that the existence of such churches has a very long history and tradition), do not recognise the validity of an ordination made by human hand, but rather that which is quaintly expressed by the phrase 'the ordination of the nail-pierced hands'. Such an ordination, being a Spirit-anointing for a task, is first recognized by the church as it responds to the functions that the 'God-called' man or woman begins to express, and is further recognized in some public way when Spirit-filled leaders of a community also confirm those gifts (cf Acts 6.3,8).

Paul recognizes the Holy Spirit's rights and prerogatives in ordination when he writes concerning the prophecies that led to Timothy being set apart for the work God had called him to do. Timothy's ministry was already acknowledged in Lystra and Iconium when Paul encouraged him to leave that area and travel with him (Acts 16.1–3). There were good reports of Timothy from the believers, so his commitment and gifts were recognized, not conferred. That the Holy Spirit and its gifts were sometimes communicated by 'laying on hands' is indisputable. 1 Tim 4:14 speaks of the elders laying hands on Timothy, as Paul also did (2 Tim 1.6). While they recognized Timothy's gifts, there was also an added impartation of the Spirit's gifting, but there is evidence in Acts 16 that Timothy already experienced God's working through him before this.

In the days of Jesus there were men who never sought public recognition and authentication of their ministries and yet were accepted by him. A spirit of bureaucratic officialdom rose up in John when he met such a man ministering without credentials: 'We forbade him to cast out demons', John reported to Jesus, 'because he is not one of us' (Lk 9.49, 50). In response, our Lord did not seek to persuade the man to join John's 'denomination' by a mutually acceptable ordination to bring him into the three-fold ministries approved by the church and so regularize the man's ministry! Rather he admonished John, and all those of the same mind as John, both then and in the church today, by stating that 'whoever is not against you is for you' and therefore for your benefit. Obedience to this injunction of Jesus has been very limited in the two thousand years of church history. Instead, it has been assumed that if you are not ordained by us you are against us and certainly we are against you. Yet John's own appointment to the twelve was Christ-ordained, not man-ordained.

Jesus himself never sought recognition from the God-appointed structures of the old dispensation. The carpenter of Nazareth seemed a little careless, if not cavalier, about seeking the High Priest's approval, let alone a certificate of ordination! If John the apostle's words (1 Jn 4.17) 'in this world we are like him' mean what they seem to mean, then a certain modelling on Jesus' practice would not come amiss. To the twelve, Jesus says: 'As the Father has sent me, I am sending you' (Jn 20.21). There is no doubt that the twelve stand in a unique position to Jesus and indeed within the church. But for the authors of *Baptism, Eucharist and Ministry* (WCC, Geneva 1982, 10) then to suggest that this has little or no relevance to the ordained ministries today is perhaps taking it a little bit too far. For indeed the apostles were told to teach future disciples all that the Lord had commanded them (Mt 28.20) and this surely must include the command to be sent forth as he had been sent forth himself. Therefore, as we look at ministries today, at least some example or relevance must be found which reflects the ministries of both Jesus and the apostles. Any commissioning whether of the twelve or of ourselves, must be rooted in Jesus and his own example, not in our own imaginations and expediencies.

Jesus' Example

What factors, then, were involved in Jesus' ordination? They were:

(1) *His own awareness* of who he was and what he had come to do in God's order (Heb 10.7).

(2) *God's testimony* to the validity of this awareness given at Jesus' baptism (Lk 3.22).

(3) *Jesus' humble submission* to God's previous charismatic and inspirational order (Mt 3.13–15). Jesus did not submit to the priestly, institutional order of robes, and the physical succession in the Old Testament priesthood. Instead he chose the order of John the Baptist, whose authority was only recognizable by the Holy Spirit's perception in the hearts of the people and was not institutionally conferred or indeed approved of. However, it was to this ordinance alone that Jesus was willing humbly to submit in his baptism, when he insisted

that John baptize him in order that he (Jesus) might fulfil all righteousness. Later, Jesus seems to put his own authority in the same nature and category as that of John the Baptist.

Jesus entered the temple courts and while he was teaching, the chief priests and the elders of the people came to him. 'By what authority are you doing these things?' they asked. 'And who gave you this authority?' Jesus replied, 'I will also ask you one question. If you answer me, I will tell you by what authority I am doing these things. John's baptism – where did it come from? Was it from heaven, or from men?' They discussed it among themselves and said, 'If we say, "From heaven", he will ask, "Then why didn't you believe him?" But if we say, "From men" – we are afraid of the people, for they all hold that John was a prophet.' So they answered Jesus, 'We don't know.' Then he said, 'Neither will I tell you by what authority I am doing these things' (Mt 21.23–27).

If the chief priests and the elders would not recognize the moral and spiritual authority of John as a God-sent minister, neither would they be abe to recognize the authority of Jesus. This challenge was the only help he gave them in answering the question. He did not say that they or the people were so simple and uninstructed that they needed a hierarchical succession to keep them in the truth. We might infer from this that neither would he have set up such a structure for the later generations of God's people, and that includes today.

(4) *Jesus' submission* to the Scriptures, which testified of him, and indeed which he heard spoken from heaven in the words of his Father, 'You are my Son, whom I love. With you I am well pleased' (Lk 3.22).

(5) *The people of God* recognized that God was with Jesus (Jn 3.2). Even among those whose standing among God's true people might be questionable (like Nicodemus at the time), there was still a popular intuitive understanding that what Jesus did and stood for was godly. In other words, good reports of him came from those who were outside the community of God's people (cf 1 Tim 3.7).

73

Jesus is known as the Christ — that is, the anointed one. This was not a title of human appointment to an office, performed by using oil for consecration as an Old Testament priest would have been anointed. It was a divine description of a task — the task of world salvation and the anointing was not with oil, but with God's Spirit himself. Although titles were offered and asked of Jesus, he never used them for himself, except for the enigmatic title 'Son of Man'. Likewise he taught his disciples to eschew titles and religious robes or dress that might appear to parade position (Mt 23.5, 8–11). Pretensions of status might destroy humility and foster pride, bringing a fall. The calling to be a minister, that is a servant, was the highest you could receive and a humble heart, not an institutional authority, was necessary for its fulfilment. No doubt the turning of Christian service to Christian domination has contributed to the popular misunderstandings of 'entering the church', when men go into ministry, as though the body of believers was not the 'real' church and as if it were not the body that served, but certain elite officials. Hierarchical or priestly structures provided a career ladder for religious aspirants to climb. There is perhaps no sin more ugly than that of trading an advance in holiness for an advance in status and position or of confusing the two. At least so it seems for those who follow the carpenter of Nazareth. The third century equating of the New Testament ministry with the Old Testament priesthood, advanced particularly by Cyprian, led to preferment, competition and in the next century to the inevitable exclusion of women from such ministry by the Synod of Laodicea in 365 AD: Canon XI states '*Presbytides*, as they are called, or female presidents are not to be appointed in the church'. A later commentator, Balsamon, writes 'In old days certain venerable women sat in Catholic churches, and took care that the other women kept good and modest order. But from their habit of using improperly that which was proper, either through their arrogance or through their base self-seeking, scandal arose. Therefore the Fathers prohibited the existence in the Church thereafter of any more such women as are called presbytides or presidents . . .' This ruling implies that women were publicly recognized as serving in the church until the fourth century, and, of course, that the men were never arrogant or self seeking in *their* behaviour!

Ordination of Women

The early church shows that there was inspirational freedom for the Spirit to raise up women in ministry. In the early years the ministry of women was recognized and stated publicly (ordained). It was in later years that male bureaucracy and hierarchy − a common failure of that gender − arose and put down women's service. Female ministry was obviously recognized in some parts of the church until this time. If we have imposed a later, heavy view of church authority onto our simple New Testament church order of serving then we have created an ordination problem when it comes to women's ministry. If, on the other hand, we are seeking to work within the simple structures of the Jesus/apostolic-style church, the inspirational, intuitive expression of service from women will be gladly received and, of course, recognized and stated so that they may function more effectively and freely. In Rom 16:7 Junia is called an apostle and in Rom 16:1 Phoebe is called a 'deacon' or minister. However, their stated position or office is described in masculine terms. Might not the same apply to other offices, e.g. elder/bishop? Clearly Paul had no problem concerning any authority these women may thereby seem to carry, probably because in the New Testament the word authority is rarely used in connection with church order.

(1) *Paul knew* that in a society of volunteers it is only a moral and spiritual authority that matters. There is no force with which to back up an institutional authority.

(2) *Paul knew* the Scriptures, and that Deborah, Miriam and Huldah were called out and ordained of God and carried authority to which men submitted.

(3) *Paul required* that his converts recognized and submitted to his fellow workers, some of whom were women, e.g. Priscilla, Tryphena, Tryphosa, Persis, Euodia, Syntyche: 'I urge you, brothers, to submit to such as these and to everyone who joins in the work, and labours at it' (1 Cor 16.16).

(4) *Phoebe*, the minister, was described by Paul in Rom 16:2 as exercising 'great help' (NIV). This is the normal word for 'lead', (Greek. *prostatis*). This gift mentioned in Rom 12:8 is used for elders ruling in 1 Tim 5:17 and 1 Thess 5:12.

For Paul, the ordination of women in ministry would simply be recognizing an already functioning ministry, in the same way as he did for men.

Paul's Example

How then did Paul view his own ordination?

Paul is an example for the whole church age, in that unlike the twelve, but like us, he arrived on the scene after the founding and ordering of the church. He also:

(1) had his own awareness of his calling (Acts 9.6; 13.2);

(2) had God's attestation of his calling (Acts 9.15; 26.13–18);

(3) had clear approval by the current church and its leadership, to which he submitted (Gal 2.9). Peter, James and John did not ordain by laying hands on Paul but simply gave him the 'right hand of fellowship';

(4) clearly submitted himself and his message to the current Scriptures and apostolic doctrine (1 Cor 15.1–5; Gal 2.2–9);

(5) was recognized by the people as having God with him, as may be seen by his reception by both Jewish and Gentile believers, without as yet the approval of Peter and the apostles in the more formal sessions of Galatians 2 or Acts 15 (see also Acts 9.13–17, 25, 27; 13.43).

Paul was at pains to make it clear that his calling, recognition, ministry and message were firstly from God and only later recognized by the apostles who offered him the right hand of fellowship and regularized and defined his ministry.

One of the evidences of a ministry ordained and empowered by God is its willingness to submit to other God-appointed ministries, as with Jesus to John the Baptist and Paul to the apostles in Jerusalem. However, equally, Paul was willing to withstand Peter openly when he felt he was compromising (Gal 2.11–21). Notice that the passage makes it very clear that Paul confronted Peter to his face in an honourable way, and certainly did not speak or write against him behind his back (Jas 4.11), which seems to be a growing practice today.

'Stated' Ministry

Paul claims that his example is incumbent upon all believers for all times and urges us to be imitators of himself (1 Cor 4.16, 17; 11.1) in the same way as he himself is an imitator of Christ whom we are all called to follow. Consequently there are those of us in the church who reason that we too must follow Jesus' and Paul's way in the matter of ordination and in following our calling and anointing by God. We believe that our gifts and function will be recognized in some way by the congregation of God's people that they have been given by God and then this will be publicly recognized or acknowledged (we prefer not to use the word 'ordained') by the currently accepted ministries. This will be either by the laying on of hands (Acts 6.6), by the right-hand of fellowship (Gal 2.9) or simply by making an announcement of some kind (Mk 3.13–19). Paul himself 'appointed' elders in Acts 14:23. These appointments were made some time after the churches had been founded, which allowed time for leadership gifts to emerge.

Acts 13:1–4 is hardly Paul's ordination for ministry, however some may argue that this was his ordination for his missionary status and it does illustrate some of the points already made. Paul and Barnabas already knew that God had called them (v 2) before the Spirit made it public, either by a prophetic word, or an intuitive communication to the leaders. Subsequently the church 'let them go' (v3) while the Spirit 'sent them out' (v4). The freedom to move in the Spirit is paramount in the story, rather than the right of the church or its officials to govern, allow or ordain. It seems that there is a value in the 'laying on of hands', 'the right hand of fellowship' or 'appointing' with the hand or through statements. That value, however, is only in the spiritual impartation which the people doing the appointing are able to bestow to aid the function of the new worker/leader. Paul fasted and prayed and then appointed elders in the churches (Acts 14.23). These churches had already been functioning for some six months, giving time for gifts to emerge and then he commended the aspiring leaders to the grace of God. The spiritual impartation to these appointees would be channelled through Paul and Barnabas' openness to God, sometimes releasing gifts, as in 2 Tim 1:6 and 1 Tim 4:14, but those gifts are of God's choosing (1 Cor 12.1). John the Baptist's fasting and prayer could well be the reason why, at Jesus' baptism, God used John at this outpouring of the Holy Spirit and not a spiritually dead Annas or Caiaphas. Just as baptism and the Lord's table are a means of grace if entered into by faith and with Spirit-filled men and women who fast and pray, so too anointing with oil and the laying on of hands (or whatever outward sign is used to state the already functioning ministry), may be used by God as a means of imparting grace. So in Acts 13:2−3 the Antioch church had commended Paul and Barnabas to the grace of God. Subsequently Paul and the elders did the same with Timothy (1 Tim 4.14; 2 Tim 1.6).

Local Church Responsibility

The ordination of elders in the Galatian churches of Acts 14 clearly suggests that the degree of responsibility is being defined. Namely, each church had its own group of elders or bishops, as in Phil 1:1 and Acts 20:17 (it was always team leadership, not a lone individual). Leaders were meant to function in mutuality and accountability to each other. Phil 1:1, Tit 1:5 and Acts 20:17,28 also indicate the equivalence of the terms elders and bishops. Elders, then, would be ordained for responsibility in a church of a given area. Their pastoral, teaching, evangelistic and prophetic *ministries* could be used and accepted everywhere in the body of Christ, e.g. Agabus (Acts 11.28: 21.10), Judas and Silas (Acts 15.32), Apollos (Acts 18.24–28), but their *responsibility* would be local, in one area only. This gives meaning to the phrase that they must have the recognition of those who are outside the church. I personally prefer and use the word responsibility rather than authority. Responsibility is what belongs to stewards and servants when authority is delegated to them. The authority imparted by Jesus to the twelve apostles was to preach, to heal and to cast out demons (Mt 10.1). Similarly effective authority in the local church is that which can control Satan's activities rather than simply control men and women. However an elder or a bishop is called and appointed for a local area, their responsibility includes the exercise of discipline. In Mt 18:15–20, this is the discipline of exclusion. This task could not have extended beyond the area in which the elder was known and publicly recognized by the flock. This may be seen in the words of our Lord 'tell it to the church' (v 17), and must refer to the local representatives of the church or to the whole church in that area, for any but those who are local could not possibly judge a matter fairly and informatively. It would appear that 'delivering someone to Satan for the destruction of the flesh' (1 Cor 5.1–5) is the supernatural aspect of the physical exclusion in church discipline, where God confirms the church's decision.

God's Recognition of Paul's Ordination

Paul's ordination by God was recognized, not conferred, by his fellow apostles and by the churches and the converts to whom he preached and wrote. It should be the same for us today. This recognition seemed to create a sphere of apostolic influence, particularly through the churches of Paul's own planting. In 2 Cor 10:8 he speaks of the authority – spiritual authority – God gave him to build up his converts and not to destroy them, and that influence was his sphere of ministry, Although he wanted always to extend it, he did not wish to take over another person's sphere or territory (vv 13,15,16). So God gives ministries which will gain spheres of influence as with Paul, but into which others such as Apollos or Peter will be welcomed (1 Cor 3.21, 22). Any invasions into other people's work will be done in the same humble and courteous spirit as Paul is advocating, not by hierarchical and bureaucratic decrees. The same spiritual and inspirational function is recorded in those passages of the Bible concerned with territorial influence and indeed with the areas of appointment. Bishops/elders (and by parallel deacons), are restricted in administrative responsibility for a given area. Apostles, prophets, evangelists, pastors and teachers may be used in their ministries in any part of the church where they are recognized and wanted, but any sense of appointment or ordination for the whole church seems to be missing in New Testament days. Officialdom did not exist, but spiritual acknowledgement of a ministry did. This, of course, opens the door for false apostles but Paul didn't think that the answer to such problems was a hierarchical arrangement to preserve order and orthodoxy (see 2 Cor 11.2−6, 13). Rather he goes on in the same chapter to show that authenticity is in a Christ-like spirit and practice of ministry. We do ill to think we know better by instituting hierarchies which crush the church into paralysis, rather than letting it grow. In those churches planted by Paul and his contemporaries their influence would have been expected and they would have felt a moral responsibility to guide the church if things were going wrong. But even then Paul would have said that he didn't want to lord it over their faith. Any kind of authority recognized was only moral and spiritual, not institutional.

How the Apostles Chose New Leaders

The recognition and subsequent stating of a ministry in the church is exemplified by the situation in Acts 1. Judas, had defected from his oversight (literally 'place of service') and 'apostleship' (Acts 1:25). Who was to take Judas' place and fill this gap in the original twelve-fold representation of the patriarchs of the new people of God, and establish the apostolic doctrine? In Acts 1:21–22 the eleven apostles' criteria for selection are clearly spelled out, along with the fact that they initially recognized the need for a new leader. So firstly, it is pointless to recognize a leader whom the rest of the leadership could not approve, or with whom they could not work. Secondly, the disciples had to be sure that such a man was truly a shepherd, since otherwise the flock would not have followed him. There is simply no point in appointing a shepherd that the sheep don't recognize. Finally, God had a say in the matter! (Acts 1.24,26). All three aspects must be taken into account when recognizing leaders of any sort in the church. It should incorporate: (1) the leaders' self-perpetuating succession; (2) congregational authority, for the Spirit indwells the body and (3) the fact that in the final analysis leaders are appointed by God. It is something recognized both by appointees and deity.

The Jesus-style Church and its Offices

These three criteria should have governed the church and its destiny of dynamic, organic, world-wide growth. Because world-wide discipleship is the God-appointed goal for the church (Mt 28.18–20) then the embracing of these principles alone would have ensured the minimum of structures and would have given the Spirit the greatest scope within the growing Church to fulfil his purpose without restriction. These loose, informal, relationship-based structures for the church in the Acts onwards were anticipated by Jesus' own ministry and training as described in the Gospels. Some critics think that Jesus didn't talk church or even plant one simply because they measure the word 'church' by some of the present unwieldy, hierarchical, career structures, which are more like international companies than fellowships of friends (Acts 27.3). However, Jesus did talk about and initiate a lightly structured fellowship movement which he called church (Mt 16.18; 18, 17). He gathered about him twelve disciples and then seventy. This movement was led by the Holy Spirit in the same way that Jesus was, and was so indwelt and filled by his presence that the danger of error and the emergence of false apostles are counteracted by the presence of God. Jesus, by his Spirit, is the greatest maintainer of orthodoxy and the least restrainer of world-wide growth and spiritual depth. His Spirit is called the 'Spirit of truth' (Jn 14.16,17) and 'guides into all truth' (Jn 16.13).

Presumably any calling from God will last as long as the God who gave it intends it to last. So similarly our recognition (ordination) would last as long also. He alone must rescind it. I suppose we may wish to retire (priests did in the Old Testament, but there is no mention of retirement in the New!). In that case, if God allows us to, we should formally and publicly state our intention. However, I would rather keep going until the coming again of Jesus and the recovery of the five-fold ministries which may precede this event!

Recovery of the Five-fold Ministries

The rise and recovery of the five-fold ministries of apostles, prophets, evangelists, pastors and teachers of Eph 4:11 are necessary, for the church to attain its full stature in its breadth and depth, expressing the unity of the Spirit in the bond of peace (Eph 4.13) and coming to the unity of the faith so that the end may come and Jesus return (Eph 4.13). This five-fold ministry will be best restored and facilitated, not by men and women presumptuously trying to create by ordination such gifts to the church but by the church crying out to God for more apostles like Paul, and for more of us to become like Ananias (Acts 9.10) and Barnabas (9.27) who can recognize these people when they arrive. Any other provision than this will mean crippling bureaucracy demanding submission to man-made (but not Jesus-made) structures called bishops, priests and deacons, having, as we understand it, no scriptural authority and often filled with men more concerned with apostolic succession than with apostolic doctrine. Together with the early church we are called and required by God to follow the apostolic doctrine and God-given men and women who are raised up by the Spirit of God to lead the church in these exciting days.

Conclusion

Some of us ask for understanding and indulgence from our brothers and sisters as we seek to practise the Master's mind as we see it, rejecting in our ministry those things Jesus never clearly commanded. We pray for all our brothers and sisters, whom we love, throughout all the man-made structures of ecclesiasticism, including our own, that we might together soon come to the day of the apostles, prophets, evangelists, pastors and teachers, and by the help of the Spirit of God might reach our full stature of maturity and of the Son of God and see in our own time the good news preached in all the world out of the true spiritual unity God has given us (Jn 17.11). This is not an artificial, man-made unity, created by the recognition of a three-fold structure of bishops, priests and deacons, but a unity which Christ prayed for, which he paid the price on the cross to create and which he gives us by the gift of his Spirit, by whose power we can fulfil his purpose for this kind of church in our own day. *Maranatha!*

6. Abolishing the laity
An Anabaptist perspective

Alan Kreider

In 428 Pope Celestine I was not amused. Honoratus, an influential monk, had just become bishop of Arles. Now news was arriving in Rome that Honoratus, to the Pope's 'astonishment', had as bishop been wearing clothing that differentiated him from laypeople. This, Celestine declared, was contrary to tradition. Not only was it a 'novelty'; it was also a 'superfluous superstition.' It was right that the clergy be distinguished from 'the common folk', as well as from non-Christian people. But let this be 'by our learning, not by our garments; by our mode of life, not by what we wear; by purity of thought, not by peculiarities of dress.'[1]

It is not hard to sympathize with Honoratus. By the late fourth century the Roman clergy, according to their pagan critics, were 'enriched with gifts from matrons, go about seated in carriages, (and) are clothed in style.'[2] Yet earnest clerics like Honoratus, in their impulse towards an ecclesiastical anticipation of the school uniform, were attempting by their example to win the higher clergy over to a simple lifestyle. Perhaps this, in part, was why Celestine's letter, the first reported mention in church history of clerical costume for secular clergy, had such meagre results. Not for the first time, a papal intervention failed to stop, or even delay, an unwanted innovation. By the end of the fifth century innumerable priests were dressing in a distinctive, archaic manner that was no longer reserved for monks.[3] But there must have been other reasons for this spread of ecclesiastical attire, reasons to which Celestine was sensitive. Although he assumed that there would be distinctions between clerics and layfolk, he was concerned that these not be unnecessary – or too visible. In this way, by resisting something which, to us, seems an obvious component of a clerical lifestyle, Pope Celestine was being conservative. He was holding to some of the earliest traditions of the church at a time when those traditions were withering.

Others in Rome were aware of these early traditions. Amidst a general rush towards aristocratic clericalism, there were those who remembered that many parts of the church had once been characterized by a 'universal ministry.'[4] The pseudonymous Pauline scholar Ambrosiaster, writing a generation before Celestine, recalled: 'At first, all taught and baptized on whatever days and seasons occasion required . . . That the people might grow and multiply, it was at the beginning permitted to all to preach the gospel, and to baptize, and to explain the scriptures in church.' But subsequently things had changed 'when the church embraced all places, houses of assembly were constituted, and rulers and the other offices in the church were instituted.' To Ambrosiaster's tidy mind this came as a great relief, for 'when all do everything, that is irrational, vulgar and abhorrent.'[5]

In Rome, thus, there were traditions and memories which pointed back to an earlier church, a pre-Christendom church. These memories were, to be sure, overschematized. As I shall point out, the early Christian congregations were not uniform – it was rarely if ever the case that 'all did everything.' But these memories pointed back to church as that had been animated by different values from those in ascendancy by the late fourth century. Throughout church history these memories have remained controversial. Are these memories consistent with a faithful reading of the biblical texts? Do the early documents of the post-apostolic church indicate that something radical was afoot? And, in any event, what relevance do origins have to Christians living many centuries later, in very different circumstances?

My own conviction, reading the Bible and church history from an Anabaptist perspective, is that there is life in the roots. In a post-Christendom world, we are most likely to get genuinely relevant insight from sisters and brothers living in an era before the church grew through inducement and compulsion, not least because inducement and compulsion are, I believe, antithetical to true Christianity. For this reason, in thinking about ordination, we are likely to benefit by pondering the insights of one of the earliest documents of the church in Rome. 'You,' 1 Pet 2.9 informed communities of believers in Asia Minor, 'are a royal priesthood . . . God's own people (*laos*).'

Where might Peter (or a close associate writing in his name) have got this cojoining of universal priesthood and universal peoplehood? It is not improbable that Peter heard something similar from the man whom he had left his nets to follow and who was the fount of the movement to which Peter had given his life. Jesus of Nazareth's brief public career was marked by the confidence that ordinary people, who knew God as Abba and were animated by God's Spirit, could do great things. Possibly for this reason, his career was also characterized by conflict with professional religionists. Peter must certainly have remembered the tense occasion upon which Jesus, in the remarkable scene recorded in Mt 23, pronounced his multiple 'Woes' upon the teachers and renewal leaders of his day. They, said Jesus, were behaving oppressively and ostentatiously; they were enjoying honorific titles and wearing distinctive garb. But, turning to his followers, Jesus said, in effect, 'Don't be like them!' 'You are not to be called rabbi . . . Call no one your father on earth . . . Nor are you to be called instructors' (Mt 23.8–11). Instead, Jesus gave to his followers their true identity – they are God's children; they are brothers and sisters; they are his disciples. And, because of all of this, they are servants.

Servanthood. That was Jesus' understanding of his own mission (Mk 10.45). That also, according to Jesus, was the destiny of his disciples. And it was a lesson which they had the greatest difficulty in learning. Repeatedly, using instructional aids (such as a child) and speaking with great asperity,

Jesus warned his followers against exercising the forms of power characteristic of Gentile leaders. Instead, he called them to be, and to think of themselves as being, servants (e.g., Mk 9.35; 10.43; Lk 22.25-26). On the last night of his life, Jesus re-emphasized this vocation by interrupting the Passover seder to enact a mnemonic ceremony which he then gave to his disciples – reciprocal footwashing. 'If I, your Lord and Teacher, have washed your feet, you also ought to wash one another's feet' (Jn 13.14). Jesus' followers – all of them – were to be servants. The earliest Christian writers reflected upon and applied these themes which they had heard – and heard reported – from Jesus. They also appropriated and universalized themes which they had gleaned from the Old Testament (e.g. Ex 19.6). These themes emphasized the common properties of all Christians. The members of the Christian communities were all, as children of one Father, brothers and sisters. They were all disciples – apprentices – of Jesus. As they learned from him, they were all distinctive, all saints. As recipients of the Holy Spirit, they all had gifts and ministries. By God's grace they were all the people (*laos*) of God; but at the same time they were also all a priesthood. They all were members of Christ's body. In keeping with Jesus' passionate desire, all of them – without exception – were servants.

They had entered into this common ministry by baptism, through which they had moved from death to life, from old social solidarities to a new order of relationships and commitments rooted in the Kingdom of God. Through the laying-on of hands, they had been commissioned to a life of ministry, entered into a new order, and experienced 'ontological change'. And they had been empowered for this new life of service by the outpouring of the Holy Spirit of God. For them baptism was thus ordination.[6]

In three seminal passages (Rom 12.4–13; 1 Cor 12.7–11; 12.27-30), Paul gave sample lists of the diverse gifts that, through the Holy Spirit's work, were apportioned among all the disciples of Jesus for ministry. These gifts ranged widely across the life of God's people: from prophecy to hospitality, from uttering wisdom to interpreting tongues. Paul was explicit that these were various forms of *service*; and, as manifestations of the Spirit, they were given to everyone ('to each') or the good of all. The ministry, in a Pauline community, was universal, for every member.

In his lists of gifts and ministries, Paul included gifts of leadership. In two passages, Rom 12 and 1 Cor 12.7–11, Paul scattered these in the midst of a sampling of many gifts. In two other passages, however, these gifts seem to have had functional priority: in 1 Cor 12.28 Paul noted that 'God has appointed in the church first apostles, second prophets, third teachers,' after which Paul noted other gifts that had been apportioned to members of the body of Christ; and in Eph 4.11 Paul mentioned apostles, prophets, evangelists, pastors and teachers without noting other gifts. The latter two passages indicate the importance that Paul ascribed to these ministries for the establishment and maintenance of Christian communities; but the former two remind us that these gifts of designated leadership were no more spiritually exalted than other gifts (e.g. exhorting, giving, healing, assisting). Paul was adamant about this: the parts of the body that seemed weaker were indispensable and worthy of 'greater honour' so that all the members 'may have the same care for one another' (1 Cor 12.22–25). There was thus, in these early Christian communities. an 'egalitarian ecclesiology (which) in no way excluded leadership and authority.'[7]

This delicate interdependence of gifts – leadership gifts along with other ministries – is well stated in Eph 4. Paul was concerned to remind his readers that, by virtue of one baptism, grace was given 'to each of us' (4.5, 7). To some members of the community, who probably constituted a kind of leadership team, Christ had given gifts of apostleship, prophecy, evangelism, pastoring and teaching. The purpose of these gifts, however, was to equip the other gifted community members to do their 'work of ministry' and thereby to build up the multigifted corporateness which is the body of Christ.[8] 'The full stature of Christ' (4.13) was thus not realized by individual members; it was realized when the entire body functioned in what Mennonite theologian John Howard Yoder has called a 'divinely coordinated multiple ministry.'[9] In this fullness, the role of the designated leaders was to serve the community by enabling every member to find his or her distinctive service.

It is not clear how this worked in practice. It is likely that teaching and preaching and even baptizing could be done by many members. As Anglican liturgical scholar Paul Bradshaw has pointed out:

> *It was the privilege and responsibility of every baptized Christian to be a minister of Christ in accordance with the mutual discernment of gifts, and so liturgical participation in the ministry of word and prayer would be open to all whose gifts were recognized by the community.*[10]

The same was probably true of presiding at communion; there is no evidence to suggest that only designated leaders could preside over the table eucharists.[11] And yet there were needs – of planting and linking churches, of uttering messages from God, of exercising spiritual responsibility and authority – which existed in all emerging communities. At first these seem to have been functions rather than offices; 1 Thess 5.12, in which Paul speaks of those who 'labour among you, and care for you (*proistamenous*) in the Lord and admonish you', contains no job titles.[12] Indeed, one of the most commonly used designations of early Christian leaders – *synergoi* (co-workers) – reveals much about the functioning of the early Christian leaders (e.g. Rom 16.3, 9; Phil 4.3). By working together, by synergizing, they achieved more than they could have done by solo performing.

Within a few years, in many churches, titles emerged to describe the leadership functions that were necessary to enable communities of ministers to flourish. Apostles, prophets, evangelists soon were mentioned by job title; so also were persons who exercised enabling and oversight (pastors, elders, bishops); and so, eventually, were people who in various ways helped the other leaders – these were given the title *diakonoi* (servants), which, however, in essence was the calling of every member of a community of servants. Almost invariably in the New Testament these terms are listed in the plural; in early Christianity there is no thought of monopastoring. Sometimes these servants were paid by their communities; at other times they earned their own keep. Often women seem to have been involved with men, in many types of ministry (including that of apostleship, prophecy, leading of house-churches and 'co-working' (synergism)).[13] There is little information about how these gifts were discerned and these ministries accredited. Several passages refer to an 'appointing' which was done, in new communities by apostles acting autonomously, and in more mature communities by corporate decision-making (Acts 14.23; 6.5; 2 Cor 8.19). This appointing was accompanied by prayer and laying-on-of-hands, a channel of blessing which the early Christians used in baptism and on many other occasions.[14]

In the milieu of the ancient Mediterranean world, a religious community shaped like this must have seemed countercultural. Christianity's main rivals were served by paid professionals, whether rabbinic teachers or priests of Asclepius or Cybele; these all had their distinctive titles and characteristic vestments. But the Christians, who in their attempt to be faithful to Jesus did many curious things, were accustomed to viewing themselves as strangers in their societies. A common self-designation of Christians was 'resident aliens' (*paroikoi*). This reminded them that whereas they could be relatively at home anywhere, they could be absolutely at home only in heaven.[15]

As the centuries went by, however, the early Christians, losing the vision of Rom 12.2, gradually became conformed to their environment. This accommodation was as prevalent in the area of ministry as it was in other areas of their life. It was not that the ministry of all believers disappeared; indeed, the spread of Christianity was the product of the witness and common life of countless anonymous believers.[16] In late second century Gaul, Irenaeus of Lyons asserted that all Christians have the 'sacerdotal order'.[17] And some years later in Caesarea, Origen urged his hearers to realize that 'the priesthood has been given to you also, that is to the whole church of God and the nation of believers.'[18]

Nevertheless, changes were soon evident that indicate that the Christian movement was losing sight of the 'universal ministry'. At differing paces from place to place, the churches were developing a distinctive corps of leaders, who alone would have titles and accreditation and who increasingly would dominate the church's ministries. A significant early indication of this is the appearance, in Clement of Rome's letter of AD 96 to the 'resident aliens' in Corinth, of the word *laikoi*, which in contrast to leaders now meant 'laity' – a term which was to have a great future.[19] The designated leadership of the Christian communities gradually became standardized. As the apostles died out and prophets lost vision and voice, Christian communities were led by bipartite (bishops and deacons) or tripartite (bishops, presbyters and deacons) teams. By AD 215, these positions were implicitly ranked in a career structure; a deacon, by 'serving blamelessly and purely . . . may attain the rank of a higher order.'[20] Meanwhile, certain functions, such as teaching and presiding at the eucharists, were limited to members of specific 'orders' of what were now known as *kleros* ('clergy'). The orders of clergy, in similar fashion to orders in Roman political and social life, had special rights and duties by virtue of their office and status. By the end of the second century, men entering clerical orders were commissioned by a service which was now called by the Latin word *ordinatio* (ordination).[21]

It was in the fourth century, in the years following the conversion of the emperor Constantine I, that the Church took its decisive steps away from universal ministry and towards aristocratic clericalism. As Christians came to accept inducement and compulsion as recruiting devices, this became unavoidable. Through its growing alliance with the imperial power, Christianity became a religion to which it was advantageous to adhere. Church growth ensued, with huge congregations replacing the house churches of the earlier centuries. Basilicas were now crammed with people (*laikoi*). The *paroikoi*, no longer the resident aliens of 1 Peter, had become parishioners, not resident aliens but settled residents, inhabitants of the 'parishes' which, by force and fiat, had become uniformly Christian.[22] A Spirit-gifted universal ministry could hardly be expected of masses, many of whom had been press-ganged into the churches. Indeed, as a late fourth-century church order observes, it was difficult simply to ensure that during services 'nobody may whisper, slumber, laugh or nod'.[23]

Supervising these people, and ministering to them by awesome rite and rhetorical sermon, was now the calling of orders of religious professionals. As the church grew, new orders, such as 'diggers', 'doorkeepers' and 'readers', were added to what was now clearly an ecclesiastical hierarchy. Modelled upon the imperial civil service, the church's hierarchy became a career structure, in which men (women had now almost completely vanished from leadership)[24] 'advanced' from grade to grade as well as often from one congregation to another. The conversion of the bishops from the chief pastor of a Christian community to the ecclesiastical administrator of a 'diocese' containing many churches was an integral part of the emergence of hierarchy.[25] By the end of the fourth century ordination had become a sacrament, conferring indelible ontological change upon the ordinand and using 'language which might, a century earlier, have been used to describe the consequences of baptism.'[26] This change was fundamental and far-reaching. As Gregory of Nyssa put it, the ordinand's 'invisible soul is transformed by some unseen power and grace to the higher state.' 'Yesterday and before he was one of the people, one of the crowd, (but) suddenly he is revealed as a guide, a president, a teacher of righteousness.'[27] In contrast to pre-Constantinian Christianity, the fundamental division was no longer between 'Church' and 'world' it was now between 'ministers' and 'laity.'[28] It was this differentiation of priests from laypeople that made the introduction of a distinctive clerical attire, despite Pope Celestine's protests, so unstoppable.

With these developments, the post-Constantinian church's perspective on ministry had altered fundamentally from that of its earliest antecedents. This shift was best stated in the late fourth century by Ambrosiaster. Leaders, he stated, inverting

Eph 4.12, 'do the work of the church in the service of the believers;'[29] they evidently no longer saw it as their calling to elicit the distinctive service of all believers. Within the fully developed structures of Orthodox and Catholic Christianity much committed and pastorally sensitive ministry continued to take place. But this ministry took place according to different assumptions from that of early Christianity. The church's leaders were by definition servants; but their actions were often characterized by exercises of the Gentile power against which Jesus had warned his disciples (Lk 22.25−26). Preoccupied with warding off the power of lust, church leaders often forgot Jesus' warnings about the lust for power. Small wonder, in this world in which the reciprocity of ministry had withered, that the mnemonic device of footwashing either vanished altogether or survived as a patronizing gesture, in which an ecclesiastical superior ceremonially washed the feet of selected inferiors.

I have neither the space nor the competence to trace a history of the ministry − 'lay' and ordained. A few comments may, however, be in order. The Protestant Reformers of the sixteenth century protested against the clericalism of the Medieval Church. An early watchword of the Reformation was the 'priesthood of believers.' Although early in the Reformation this occasionally led to a renewed involvement by the laity in spiritual ministry, in general the Reformers interpreted priesthood theologically rather than ecclesiologically. They were more convinced, that is, that all believers have direct access to God than that all believers have a priestly ministry to each other and the world.[30] Indeed, it seems that in large measure the Protestant Reformers were content to perpetuate the structures and assumptions of the post-Constantinian church. Protestants, to be sure, now specialized in sermons and the Catholics in rites and sacraments; but both emphasized ministry as something which religious professionals do on behalf of their flocks. For a querying of these structures we must turn to renewal movements − Lollards, Anabaptists, Quakers − and to unusual individuals who believed that God was summoning them into uncharted terrain. Symbolic of these (a large number of these spiritually sensitive individuals were women) is the Anabaptist Lijsken Segers of Antwerp, to whom in 1551 her inquisitor blurted out with exasperation, 'Why do you trouble yourself with the scriptures? Attend to your sewing.'[31] Also symbolic is the better known spiritual pioneer Susannah Wesley of Epworth, whose Sunday evening prayer services excited such insecurity in her clerical spouse.[32]

Even in the so-called 'free churches' clericalist assumptions remained largely unchallenged. As Winthrop Hudson has noted:

> *The (Baptist) improvised church order . . . developed somewhat unwittingly and unconsciously, being dictated more by considerations of expediency and necessity rather than by considerations stemming from a re-examination of the nature of the church and its vocation in the world.*[33]

In other traditions, such as Methodism, there have at times been more imaginative experiments;[34] but even these have succumbed eventually to a preponderant clericalism. The mono-pastoral model − in which it is the 'ordained minister' whose ministration really count as ministry, who really can preside at communion, by whom one has really been visited − has proven to be wonderfully indestructible.

This has continued to be true even in the latter half of the twentieth century. As Western Christianity has entered a period of crisis and as previous legal and social constraints have withered, church attendance throughout Europe has plummeted. Some theologians have seen an empowering of the laity as an appropriate antidote to this. Over forty years ago Dutch theologian Hendrik Kraemer wrote *A Theology of the Laity*, in which he argued that a 'priestly-hierarchical' tradition was almost as operative in the Protestant traditions as in the Roman Catholic church. He also observed:

> *The laity or body of lay-membership of the church has never in church history enjoyed the distinction of being treated with care and thoroughness as a matter of specific theological importance or significance.*[35]

94

Partly as a result of his initiative, the World Council of Churches began its Department of the Laity. Simultaneously, Dominican scholar Yves Congar was calling Roman Catholics to recover a vision of lay ministry, intriguingly for missiological reasons. 'History shows that the apostolate of the laity is only taken seriously when a "real world" exists to confront the Church, and the Church is aware of it.'[36] Jesuit theologian Karl Rahner came to similar conclusions. In 1974 he observed that a transition was under way between the traditional state church and 'a church as that community of believers who critically disassociate themselves, in virtue of free personal decision in every case, from the current opinions and feelings of their social environment.' An essential component of this new church will be 'declericalization', in which the primary impetus for life will come 'from below.'[37] Meanwhile, in North America, Methodist ecclesiologist Howard Snyder has for many years, in numerous books and articles, been calling the church to become 'a community of ministers.'[38]

But change has been slower than many have desired. After years of work to help churches in 'the rediscovery of the laity,' Hans-Ruedi Weber of the World Council of Churches has commented ruefully, 'Church structures proved to be much more difficult to renew than we had expected.[39] As he must recognize, the 'Lima Document' on *Baptism, Eucharist and Ministry* devotes ten times as much space to 'The Church and the Ordained Ministry' as it does to 'The Calling of the Whole People of God.'[40] I doubt that this is because, as one ecumenical apologist has argued, the churches, agreeing on the importance of the ministry of the laity, chose to devote space to topics about which they disagreed.[41] It is rather, I suspect, because it would require re-education and repentance, on the part of many people, to repudiate the structures and assumptions of clericalism. In the apt words of Weber, it would require 'a Copernican change.'[42]

This, I believe, is what must happen. To be responsive to the vision of the New Testament and the needs of our time, Christians must stop seeing the ecclesiastical universe in clerico-centric terms. No longer will it do to think in terms of ministers as distinct from laity, of higher-ups and lower-downs. Instead, when thinking of ministry, Christians must think of the services offered by every gifted believer. No longer content with feeble and often patronizing attempts to emancipate lay people, Christians must commit themselves to dismantling a two-tier church. Christians are used to talking about *the priesthood of all believers*; people assent and nothing changes. Perhaps it would help jolt our thought and action out of accustomed ruts if we altered the slogan. Our calling is nothing less than *the abolition of the laity*.

Such a change will not be easy. For the traditional structures continue precisely because they are traditional, and because Christians are 'codependent' in keeping them that way. Ordained clergy, on the one hand, are accustomed to viewing themselves as professionals. They have their training institutes, their forms of certification, their career structures. They even have their guilds, which they often call 'Fraternals'. Archbishop Runcie gave expression to this guild mentality when talking about the role of other bishops in his enthronement service: 'I will be seen to be one of a band of brothers.'[43] In the church of Christ, is it really only the clergy who are brothers? And if so, do the best insights of the sisters really motivate them to join a system as elitist as this? From their position of brotherly eminence, the clergy are accustomed to providing professional 'services' and often, in significant measure, to exercising control over the life of their churches. The nonordained laity, on the other hand, whether as faithful traditionalists or as religious consumers in a consumer society, are complicit through viewing it as their due to be served by the holy people whom they pay.

Despite this inbuilt conservatism, change is taking place. The monopastoral model is breaking down; new forms of ministry are emerging; and the clerico-centric view of the universe is less and less convincing to people who are observing what is going on in the world and the church — and who are reading their Bibles. A major force or structural change, throughout the West and in many parts of the Third World, has been stark necessity: the number of ordinands, in many traditions, has fallen dramatically. A wide variety of 'lay ministries' have sprung up as Base Ecclesial Communities have flourished. The trans-denominational charismatic movement has provided dramatic evidence that charism is not primarily channelled by linear, 'apostolic' descent. One commentator, Dutch theologian Edward Schillebeeckx, has rejoiced in these 'alternative practices.' The church's response to these, he believes, should be the recognition of 'a fourth ministry' which, working with the recognized orders of bishops, priests and deacons, would help 'as many members as possible (to) be involved in building up the church.'[44] More radical than Schillebeeckx, Reformed exegete Markus Barth has called for a 'church without laymen and priests.'[45] But how to move in this direction remains unclear. Jesuit Karl Rahner has viewed this as a time for experiment and pioneering. The German title of his influential book *The Shape of the Church to Come* expresses his hopeful outlook: *The Changing Structure of the Church as Task and Opportunity.*[46] And Rahner has offered one significant hint, 'All that we can say about the future of the Church is that whatever form its development may take, it will be consistent with its origins.'[47]

In what follows, I shall offer fourteen goals, ways forward which I believe are consistent with the church's origins and which may be useful as we reflect on ministry in the 1990s and beyond. I offer these with varying degrees of confidence. I have experienced realizations of these goals in churches with which I have been associated; but some of these goals I have not seen adequately realized anywhere. The goals that I suggest, although in keeping with much Mennonite thinking, by no means represent a cross-section of Mennonite practice in any country. I am aware of my need of instruction and reproof by the understandings and experiences of sisters and brothers in many traditions; and I recognize that there is holiness and faithful discipleship among Christians whose ecclesiological traditions differ from my own. To some of these, I recognize, many of my suggested goals may seem grossly impossible – even intrinsically objectionable. But I hope that every reader will find here at least one or two ideas worth pondering, and maybe even some goals to work toward. I sense that, as the church responds to the challenge of ministry in a post-Christendom world, more and more Christians – in many traditions – will be willing to experiment.

New patterns of ministry and new terminology are emerging. We should, I believe, greet change; but we should not welcome it uncritically. Each new development in ministry, and each suggestion that I shall make, must be tested. Does it aid the Church in its kingdom work and mission? Is it consistent with the Church's origins (is it apostolic)? And preeminently we must use Paul's criteria (Eph 4.11–13): does it equip all the saints to be servants? Does it build up the body of Christ? Does it enable the believers together to grow into a maturity that is Christ-filled and Christ-like?

Goal 1. We will increasingly view baptism as functional ordination. This idea is not new; it was stated with intense conviction in Martin Luther's earliest Reformation writings. But to me it is foundational. In baptism we testify to our repentance, dying to sin and being born to 'newness of life' (Rom 6.2–4). No longer encumbered by guilt or by old inevitabilities, we by God's gracious action are 'clothed' with Christ Jesus, in whom there is liberation from oppression and in whom 'all of you are one' (Gal 3.23–28). Through baptism we thus experience a shift in 'order' – from a solidarity with a rebellious humanity to a new solidarity with those who are one in a socially-encompassing body of nonconformists (1 Cor 12.13). It is members of this body who 'drink of one Spirit'. In Paul's thought, baptism in the Holy Spirit is conjoined with water baptism. It equips all the members of Jesus' *ordo* of disciples, gifting them for ministry (1 Cor 12.47).

Goal 2. The church will become a community of ministers.[48] Through the working of the Holy Spirit, every member of Christ's body is gifted. This gifting enables them, in their various ways, to be servants; it is 'for the work of ministry' (Eph 4.12). In the church, there are thus no non-ministers. As Howard Snyder has provocatively commented, 'In a church of one hundred members, (God) wants one hundred ministers, not one, five or ten.'[49] This understanding does not do away with a specialized ministry; on the contrary, through the diversity of the Spirit's gifting, the ministries of many members will be highly specialized. Nor does this understanding assume that every Christian's ministry will be equally responsible; in any congregation, there will be differing degrees of personal and spiritual maturity. What this understanding does away with is what Yoder has called the 'undifferentiated laity.'[50] It is worth noting that, since this understanding presupposes that the members of the church are Christian believers, it is likely to be most at home in churches that practise believers' baptism.

Goal 3. A church that is a community of ministers will find appropriate means to discern spiritual gifts. The Holy Spirit sovereignly apportions gifts, all of which are essential to the body's health, among all Christians (1 Cor 12.11). These gifts, which are breathed upon Christians, are not identical. A gifted body is egalitarian but it is not anarchic, in which any member may do anything.[51] The Spirit can change or withdraw the gifts. The work of the Spirit will best be sensed as members minister, as they serve each other and the world. It is through responding to each other's ministries truthfully that we discern the gifts that God has given to each. The church will need to become a community of truth-telling to overcome the inclination of many members to self-deception, flattery and dissimulation. This is hard; in our 'affirmative' age niceness is a beguiling temptation. But it is not impossible. As Paul commented to the Ephesians, it is by 'speaking the truth in love' that the church grows into a body in which every 'ligament' collaborates properly (4.15–16). Increasingly, congregations will discover that this truthful discernment takes place best when assisted by a thoughtfully constructed gift discernment process.[52]

Goal 4. Designated gifts of leadership will be among the spiritual gifts that will be given to any community of ministers. Paul was clear on this point: he expected that by God's grace in the church at Rome, and by implication in other churches, gifts of leading and teaching would mingle with those of faith and compassion (Rom 12.4–8). There was, for Paul, no ontological distinction between these gifts. Paul knew that there were contributions that a visitor from outside could bring to the congregation (Rom 1.11). He assumed, however, that the essential gifts for leading the congregation's life were those which God will 'raise up' within the congregation; they would not need to be 'called' from another congregation or from theological college. Today as well, the gifts of the designated leaders will be attested by the experience of the members of the congregation. Their service may well be especially appropriate to local needs, for they will intimately know the ethos of the congregation which has called them.

Goal 5. The primary calling of the designated leaders will be to enable every member to be a minister. At times congregations may wish to use biblical titles – elders, pastors, bishops, deacons. At other times, in the knowledge that these biblical terms were often adapted from first-century secular parlance, congregations may prefer to speak of members of a 'leadership team'. The titles of the designated leaders will vary; however, the plural nature of the leadership of a congregation (leadership titles in the New Testament are always plural) should not vary. What is vital is that the designated leaders carry out, on behalf of the other servant members in the congregation, four essential tasks. First of all, they must, on behalf of the congregation, take overall responsibility for its common life, and for the life of its members. Second, they must lead the congregation by articulating its common vision, and by helping all members to express this in action. Third, they must enable a 'pastoral centre' to emerge, which ensures that the congregation is a safe place, a place with a hearth.[53] But above all, they must take the lead in encouraging the ministry of others, nurturing the immature to maturity and the sick to health, thereby enabling the congregation to become a ministering priesthood.

Goal 6. The gifted ministers who are not designated leaders will nevertheless function in many ways. There is no reason that the designated leaders should do most of the teaching or worship leading. These tasks, including presiding at eucharists, are matters, not of status (who is pastor?), but of spiritual gift (through whose leadership do the people most freely learn or worship God?). The same is true of counselling, chairing congregational business meetings, hospitality, leading music in worship, administering church finances, and many other tasks. As a result, the contributions of the designated leaders, while absolutely essential to the health of a congregation, may not always be immediately visible to a casual visitor.

Goal 7. Theological and practical training will be vital in the life of a congregation of ministers. Much training can take place in the course of the normal life of the congregation, as members work and suffer, learn to pray and to understand the Bible, and carry out their various ministries. Designated leaders as well as other ministers can be well trained locally, often through being apprenticed to more experienced Christians. Theological education by extension (including correspondence courses), leadership training programmes such as Work Shop, congregation-based theological education such as that of the Northern Baptist College or the Northern Ordination Course (Anglican), or other part-time non-residential courses at theological colleges may help leaders learn while remaining in their congregations. At times it will be appropriate for people who have a special vocation to Bible study and theology and a special gift in teaching to undertake courses of study that are available at theological colleges or universities. Such residential education can put much needed resources at the disposal of congregations. But it, while appropriate, should not become the norm. More normal should be the retooling, by existing theological colleges, of their programmes to facilitate the training of leaders in the places where they are already ministering. Whatever the mode of training, the aim of training must be to produce new kinds of interactive, listening leaders who, having 'come down from the throne of knowledge and ideas and travel along the roads,' are able to prepare maps that correspond 'with the features of the land on which the people walk and suffer.'[54]

Goal 8. Women and men will minister together, at every level of the church's life. This collaboration, which seems to have characterized the Christian movement in its earliest years, should be seen as normal. It need not be invariable. Since the invariable norm of a universal ministry is that all should minister according to the gifts that God has given them, there may be times when only women or only men are ministering. It is, however, the experience of a growing number of congregations that things go best when the gifts and wisdom of both men and women operate together.

Goal 9. In a community of ministers commissioning will take place frequently. It will be appropriate to pray for and lay hands on those who are being commissioned as designated leaders. But other ministers, who are exercising other charisms for the health of the body and the witness of the church, should be commissioned in a similar way. This is not a means of establishing an 'upper class' of church members; ideally, and ultimately, all Christians, as their gifts emerge, should experience their congregation's affirmation of their ministries. What is essential is that existing ministries be recognized, blessed, and prayed for, and that they be made accountable to the congregation that they are serving. As churches discover that their priestly ministry is also exercised for the sake of the world, they may on occasion lay hands on members for demanding missions in secular employment.

Goal 10. The 'ordination' of all ministering members will be 'relative', not 'absolute'. There is no necessary reason to assume that a person who has been an effective 'overseer' or 'counsellor' or 'community involvement instigator' will continue to be equally effective in these roles forever, or if he or she should move to a different congregation. The Holy Spirit, who gives gifts, can revoke gifts. Congregations, and especially designated leaders, should be sensitive to this — alert to members who are ministering in ways that appear self-aggrandizing. Furthermore, congregations differ. It is therefore not helpful to view 'ministers' as transferable functional components. When they move to a new congregation, they should be subject to processes of gift discernment along with other members. If their gifts are affirmed, they may be re-commissioned in their new congregation.

Goal 11. 'Ministers' will avoid titles, especially titles that refer to status rather than function. All Christians, by virtue of their baptismal 'ordination', share a common status – disciples of Jesus. Since all of them are ministers, and since their services are many, titles could get tedious. If a designation of ministry is needed, 'John, Bible Study Leader' or 'Susan, Pastor' will do – provided that people remember that the 'pastor' is a member of a team of designated leaders, not the focal point of the life (and criticism) of the congregation. Titles such as 'Reverend', which presuppose distinctions of ontology and training between members of the church, should be avoided on dominical grounds (Mt 23.8–9).

Goal 12. Clerical clothing will not be worn by members of ministering communities. The same reasoning applies here as with titles of status. In a world in which pagan priests had their distinctive garb, the Early Church grew despite its lack of a visible clerical presence in society. Certainly it gives pause for thought that the Christian Church took almost four centuries after Pentecost to invent clerical attire. It is understandable that Christians who minister in hospitals or prisons should find it convenient to use clothing to indicate that they have special contributions to make; but these advantages are outweighed by the offence caused, within a church which conceives itself as a community of ministers, by giving special attire to some of them. If special attire is to be worn, let it be worn, on days of high celebration, *by everyone*! Wouldn't it be festive if, on Pentecost, we all wore red? Or on Sundays, as in some African churches, if we all wore white?

Goal 13. Congregations will provide financial support for ministering members in a flexible way that will vary according to need. Some designated leaders may have full-time jobs and support themselves and others by their labours; other designated leaders may devote all their working hours to the church. Some members with other ministries may require full- or part-time support from the church; others may make their contributions voluntarily. There is no reason why the persons who are paid by the church should be the designated leaders; and there is good reason why a congregation should not view its leader as a 'paid professional'.

Goal 14. All congregations, and teams of designated leaders, will need to be accountable, internally and externally. Internally there will be accountability of all members, including the designated leaders, to the congregation gathered for discernment and business. As congregations grow in the ministry of every member, they will simultaneously discover the importance of a regular, powerful (and therefore well-attended) business meeting.[55] It is to the other believers, as well as to God, that the designated leaders are accountable.

The other believers, each with their ministries, will be accountable to the designated leaders, who are responsible to God for the spiritual welfare of both believers and body; and recognizing this responsibility, they will accord to the designated leaders freedom to lead and to envision. Significantly, in the first major adjustment of church polity recorded in church history, decision-making was interactive, involving both designated leaders and 'the whole community' (Acts 6.1−6).

Externally as well, congregations and teams of designated leaders will need accountability. Local problems, without illumination from different experience and a wider perspective, can seem intractable. And at times a person from outside, in whom a congregation has recognized wisdom and the capacity to elicit the gifts of all believers, can bring words of healing authority into sick situations. This has been a strength in the episcopacy of the 'great traditions'. In the coming years of crisis for Western Christianity, however, I sense that all traditions – episcopal and non-episcopal – may benefit by re-examining their structures and assumptions. As they do this, thinkers in the episcopal traditions may recognize that something went awry when the church took over the administrative structures of its imperial environment; when bishops began to wear the purple which hitherto had indicated the status of the pagan magistrates; when bishops, instead of being lead pastors within a congregation or senior overseers over a small number of churches became ecclesiastical administrators over vast areas containing countless churches. These episcopal structures may have been suited to maintenance in a world in which everyone had to be Christian; but are they equally suited, in a world in which belief will be voluntary and countercultural, to mission?

Perhaps 'free church' congregations, lacking the weight of 'historic episcopacy,' can help explore ways forward to more appropriate forms of external accountability. To do this they will at times need to repent of rampant self-will masquerading as 'independence.' Forms of extra-congregational account-ability, which are often rather emaciated, have long existed in 'free church' traditions, with 'travelling evangelists,' 'area ministers' and 'superintendents.' More recently, charismatic congregations have often sought affiliation – at times loose, at times binding – to 'apostles.' North American Mennonites over the centuries have had 'bishops', always written in the lower case, senior pastors who, while rooted in the life of their own congregations, have helped guide the affairs of younger communities of faith. In Mennonite experience these 'bishops' have not always functioned in a life-giving way. Gentile power, alas, may be found in all traditions! Despite the abuses, congregations, for the sake of the emergence of their own integrity and universal ministry, will need to be accountable. Perhaps, as Baptist theologian Nigel Wright has argued, this should be to 'pastors who, while remaining in one church, become resource persons for other churches and leaders.'[56] In any event, this accountability must be interactive, in which the external leaders are shaped by their encounters with the congregations and their gifted, ministering members.

These fourteen goals may seem a mixed lot, some already the experience of many churches, and others elusive and possibly unachievable. But in all of them I am motivated by a common concern – to find structures and relationships which will enable all believers, according to the vision of Jesus and Paul, to be ministers. I am not discouraged by the fact that, from the outset, Christian churches struggled in their attempts to give life to this vision. A true vision will challenge the commitment and imagination of people in any era. And yet I am fascinated by evidences of a true memory, in which the earliest traditions of the Christian movement indicate that they were closer to realizing this vision than most of us are. I also am intrigued by the evidence of renewal movements across the centuries, and of renewal movements throughout the world today, who are giving new expression to the goal of universal ministry.

I do not think that the chief impediment to what I am proposing is tradition. There are many traditions, and the struggle for faithfulness in any era depends on how we discriminate among alternative traditions that church history – and the history of each of our denominations – offers us. To orientate ourselves truly in tradition we must ponder what God was doing as he revealed himself in his Son Jesus and began a new social movement among his followers. And as we do this we may discover a tradition that is not a manifesto for conservation but an impulse for experiment and change. As Leonardo Boff has provocatively put it, 'To preserve tradition means to do as the first Christians did.'[57]

No, the impediment to universal ministry is not so much tradition; I think it has more to do with realities of power and economic survival. The professionalised vision of ministry is so indestructible in part because its practitioners depend on it to survive. But perhaps an even more formidable blockage to universal ministry has to do with what we have come to think of as the size of a 'normal' congregation. Constantine and his successors, in first legalizing and then promoting Christianity, not only brought in new 'Christians' by means of inducement and compulsion; they also made the church big. Congregations moved from expanded sitting rooms to basilicas. And this changed everything. It put a premium on the 'ministry' of those with public, rhetorical, dramatic gift; and it relegated others, who had many forms of ministry to offer, to the status of 'passengers' in the ship of the church run by ecclesiastical 'mariners'.[58] When one person was expected to lead five hundred people in worship, professionalism was bound to arise.

Our mindsets today are conservative. Constantinianism is crumbling all around us, but we – even in 'free church' traditions – remain the captives of its values, its scale. It may be because our late-Victorian buildings determine our ecclesiology. Or it may be because, in keeping with much 'church growth' strategizing, we desire not merely that new believers be born by water and the Spirit; we, captives of an age in which statistics are the primary indicators of success, also desire big churches. With big budgets. And big people up front. How different things might be if we could conceive of 'church growth' in terms of a proliferation of member-led small congregations.

It is hard to leave behind the dominant Christendom tradition of leadership that Dutch spiritual writer Henri Nouwen bemoans:

> *One of the greatest ironies of the history of Christianity is that its leaders constantly gave into the temptation of power – political power, military power, economic power, or moral and spiritual power – even though they continued to speak in the name of Jesus, who did not cling to his divine power but emptied himself and became as we are. The temptation to consider power an apt instrument for the proclamation of the Gospel is the greatest of all.[59]*

We need big people. But we must measure their bigness by countercultural standards: are they willing to renounce 'Gentile power' (Lk 22.25)? are they true servants (Mt 23.11)? As a result of the words and work of Jesus, servanthood will henceforth be measured by the self-effacing way in which servants equip others with vision and enable them to enter into the universal ministry of those who are apprenticed to him. Ultimately it is Jesus, the giver of 'gifts to his people' (Eph 4.8), who is the measure of ministry.

I close this paper by restating a vision. It is a vision of a liberated people, each serving one another and the world through exercising the gifts that God's Spirit has given them. This is good news, and its liberating quality can be demonstrated in Christians around the world whose energies or service it has unlocked. But there is another dimension to the vision to which I have not yet alluded. It is a vision of an alternative future for a large but shrinking group of people commonly called 'ministers'. How often they are crushed by the diversity of demands made upon them by congregations who expect them to be omnicompetent. How difficult, in the midst of administration, visitation and praying at parish fetes, it is for them to discern and exercise their own life-calling and Spirit-gifting.

The early Christian vision of ministry was never that of the 'superminister'. It was of groups of ordinary people, to whom God has promised all the varied gifts necessary for them corporately to grow 'to maturity, to the measure of the full stature of Christ' (Eph 4.13). The destiny of these people was liberation, liberation to be themselves in community. This destiny is still ours to claim. To all of us it is an invitation to discover what it means to be uniquely gifted members of the servant-body of Christ.[60]

Notes

1. Celestine I, *Epistola* IV, 2 (*PL*. 50, 430–431). For comment on this document, see Léon Cristiani, 'Essai sur les origines du costume ecclésiastique,' *Miscellanea Guillaume de Jerphanion*, (Rome, 1947), 69–79.
2. Ammianus Marcellinus, *Res gestae*, 23.3.14.
3. Cristiani, 'Essai,' 76; Janet Mayo, *A History of Ecclesiastical Dress* (Batsford, London, 1984), 19.
4. I owe this term, and much more, to John Howard Yoder. *The*

Fullness of Christ: Paul's Revolutionary Vision of Universal Ministry (Brethren Press, Elgin, Illinois, 1987).

5. Ambrosiaster, *Comm. in Eph.* 4.11. 12 (*CSEL*, Ambrosiaster, III. 91, 99).

6. Markus Barth, *Ephesians*, 2 (Doubleday, Garden City, NY, 1974), 481. Barth points out that the passages in 1 Timothy's ordination to ministry, 'may well refer to the confession and laying-on-of-hands connected with baptism rather than to an antecedent of a bishop's consecration.'

7. Edward Schillebeeckx. *The Church with a Human Face* (SCM, London, 1985), 39.

8. Along with most modern commentators and translators, I assume that, for grammatical as well as theological reasons, there should be a comma after 'to equip the saints.' For a discussion of this point, see Hans-Ruedi Weber, *Living in the Image of Christ* (Judson Press, Valley Forge, PA, 1986), 70–71.

9. Yoder. *Fullness of Christ*. 16.

10. Paul Bradshaw, 'Patterns of Ministry.' *Studia Liturgica*, 15 (1982–1983), 51.

11. Schillebeeckx, *Church with a Human Face*, 72.

12. I have translated this 'care for', rather than 'have charge of' (NRSV), because I find that it better renders the nuturing, rather than dominating, function of early Christian leadership. See Bo Reicke, in *The Theological Dictionary of the New Testament VI* (Eerdmans, Grand Rapids, 1968), 701–702.

13. Rom 16.1–5, 7; 1 Cor 11.5; Col 4.15; 1 Cor 1.11; Phil 4.4. See Schillebeeckx, *Church with a Human Face*, 57; Ben Witherington III, *Women in the Earliest Churches* (CUP, Cambridge, 1988), 182, 209.

14. Everett Ferguson, 'Laying on of Hands,' in E. Ferguson, ed., *Encyclopedia of Early Christianity* (Garland Publishing, New York/London, 1990), 530.

15. 1 Pet 2.11; numerous early Christian writings cited by Pierre de Labriolle, 'Paroecia,' *Bulletin du Cange* (Archivum Latinitatis Medii Aevi), 3 (1927), 196–205.

16. Norbert Brox, 'Zur Christlichen Mission in der Spätantike,' in Karl Kertelge, ed., *Mission im Neuen Testament* (Herder, Freiburg-im-Breisgau, 1982), 226.

17. Irenaeus, *Adversus Haereses*, 4, 8, 3.

18. Origen, *Hom. in Lev.*, 10, 1.

19. I Clement, 40, 5.

20. Hippolytus, *Apostolic Tradition*, 8.

21. Tertullian, *De Idol.*, 7.

22. Labriolle, 'Paroecia,' 200–203.

23. *Apostolic Constitutions*, 2, 85.

24. There are some exceptional cases. The mid-fourth century church

order from Asia Minor called the *Testamentum Domini* (ed. J. Cooper and A.J. MacLean, T. & T. Clark, Edinburgh, 1902), reports that widows called 'presbyteresses' (*presbytidas*) stood at the front during eucharists with other ordained clergy (1.23, 35, 41–42) and engaged in ministries to women; this, however, was the apex of their ecclesiastical careers. Fifth-and sixth-century documents indicate that it is likely that women in some areas actually functioned as priests (Giorgio Otranto, 'Notes on the Female Priesthood in Antiquity,' *Journal of Feminist Studies in Religion*, 7 (1991), 78–93).

25. Everett Ferguson, 'Bishop,' in *Encylopedia of Early Christianity*, 153.

26. Bradshaw, 'Patterns of Ministry,' 55.

27. Gregory of Nyssa, *On the Baptism of Christ*.

28. Bradshaw, 'Patterns of Ministry,' 51.

29. Ambrosiaster, *Comm. in Eph.*, 4.12, 1–4 (*CSEL*, Ambrosiaster, 3, 81, 00).

30. H. Urner, 'Laiendienst,' in *Die Religion in Geschichte und Gegenwart*, 3rd ed., IV, 207; Howard A. Snyder, *Liberating the Church* (IVP, Downers Grove, Illinois, 1983), 171.

31. Thieleman Jansz Van Braght, *The Bloody Theater or Martyrs' Mirror of the Defenseless Christians who Baptized Only upon Confession of Faith* (Herald Press, Scottdale, PA, 1951), 515.

32. Adam Clarke, *Memoirs of the Wesley Family* (Lane and Tippett, New York, 1848), 387–393.

33. Winthrop S. Hudson, 'Stumbling into Disorder,' *Foundations*, I, i (April 1958), 45, cited in Paul M. Harrison, ed., *Authority and Power in the Free Church Tradition* (Princeton University Press, Princeton, 1959), 18.

35. Hendrik Kraemer, *A Theology of the Laity* (Lutterworth Press, London 1958), 9, 83.

36. Yves Conger, *Priest and Layman* (Darton Longman and Todd, London 1967), 246.

37. Karl Rahner, *The Shape of the Church to Come* (SPCK, London 1974), 23, 56.

38. This particular phrase comes from Howard A. Snyder, 'Irving Park Free Methodist Church,' in David B. Eller, ed., *Servants of the Word* (Brethren Press, Elgin, Illinois 1990), 104.

39. Weber, *Living in the Image of Christ*, 7.

40. *Baptism, Eucharist and Ministry* (WCC, Geneva 1982), 20–32.

41. Jeffrey Gros, 'Toward Unity in Faith and Universal Ministry,' in Eller, *Servants of the Word*, 187.

42. Weber, *Living in the Image of Christ*, 71.

43. *Guardian*, 29 February 1980.

44. Schillebeeckx, *Church with a Human Face*, 266.

45. Markus Barth, *Ephesians*, 2, 477.

46. Karl Rahner, *Strukturwandel der Kirche als Aufgabe und Chance* (Herder, Freiburg-im-Breisgau 1972).

47. Karl Rahner, *Theological Investigations*, cited from memory by Gerard Hughes, *Walk to Jerusalem* (Darton, Longman and Todd, London 1991), 37.

48. Howard A. Snyder, 'Irving Park Free Methodist Church,' in Eller, *Servants of the World*, 104.

49. Snyder, *Liberating the Church*, 180.

50. Yoder, *Fullness of Christ*, 46.

51. A congregation in which all members do everything because they are members is the inverse counterpart of the traditional congregation in which the 'pastor; does everything because he is pastor. Both are equally distorted, for neither takes seriously the variegated gifting of the Holy Spirit.

52. The way one parish (Holy Trinity, Wolverhampton) discerns gifts is described in *Mews from Post Green*, August 1991, 2.

53. I owe this insight to the theological vision and practical experience of Robert and Julia Banks (*The Home Church* (Lion, Tring, Herts. 1986), 107.

54. Carlos J. Mesters, *Defenseless Flower* (Orbis, Maryknoll, N.Y. 1989), 47.

55. The monthly business-meeting of the Wood Green Mennonite Church make decisions in ways that may be helpful to other congregations. See 'All Agreed, Then?,' *Adminisheet* 6 (Administry, 69 Sandridge Road, St Albans, Herts AL1 4AG).

56. Nigel G. Wright, *Challenge to Change* (Kingsway, Eastbourne 1991), 188.

57. Leonardo Boff, *Ecclesiogenesis* (Collins, London 1986), 60.

58. *Apostolic Constitutions*, 2, 58.

59. Henri Nouwen, *In the Name of Jesus* (Crossroad, New York 1989), 58.

60. This paper has benefited from the detailed criticisms of Nelson Kraybill, Stuart Murray, Dave Nussbaum, Peter Price, Christopher Rowland, and John Howard Yoder, none of whom is in agreement with me on all points. To these, and to my most committed critics Eleanor Kreider and Andrew Kreider, I want to record my gratitude.

7. Developments since Vatican II

A Roman Catholic perspective

Wilfrid McGreal

The understanding of ministry in the Roman Catholic tradition has been greatly helped by modern historical and biblical studies. The famous 'Penny' Catechism that dates from the last century and nurtured generations of English Catholics makes this solitary statement about ministry. 'Holy Orders is the sacrament by which bishops, priests and other ministers of the Church are ordained and receive power and grace to perform their sacred duties.'

In contrast to this formulation we find Herbert McCabe *New Catechism of Christian Doctrine* (Catholic Truth Society, London 1985) describing the sacrament of ministry or Orders as follows: 'By the sacrament of ministry particular members of the community are ordained to share in a special (sacramental) way in the priesthood of the Church which is the priesthood of Christ. Their function is to represent, to teach and to govern the Christian community. Their priesthood, though related to the common priesthood of the baptized, is distinct from it in being directed specifically to the ordering of the Church.' McCabe's description sees the priesthood of Christ as the core and situates the Catholic priest in the context of the priesthood of all believers and whereas the Penny Catechism stressed a cultic role, McCabe sees the priest as one who ministers to the community, especially through the role of teaching and preaching.

At the heart of the differing approaches between the catechism and McCabe, is the teaching of Vatican II, the ecumenical council held in the early 1960s which did so much to revitalise the Catholic Church and impel it into the ecumenical movement. From the early medieval period until the Vatican Council, the vision of the Catholic priest was essentially connected with the celebration of the eucharist, a cultic role. Allied with this, a spirituality for priests had developed which stressed their otherness in an extremely other worldly sense. In short, the Catholic priest had become almost a priestly caste in the Old Testament sense and was now separated from the community by dress and laws such as those that forbade them to go to the theatre. Added to that was an educational system that was separate from the universities and insulated candidates to the priesthood from the realities of contemporary life. In short, a type of monastic training was seen to be the way men would be prepared who would have to work in the local Christian community. Another aspect of the vision of the Catholic priesthood especially between 1600–1960, was an embattled stance taken against the Reformation. It was perceived that the Reformers were attacking the Catholic vision of the eucharist so the defence of Catholic teaching meant a stern resistance to anything that could compromise the faith. Of course the intolerance, prejudice and persecution that marked the sixteenth and seventeenth centuries did little to promote dialogue. However, I could in no way undervalue the heroism of the seminary priests who died for their belief in the eucharist and their ministry. My regret is that the mentality of the period prevented dialogue and that such injustice and lack of charity has lead to the weakening of Christianity in the western world.

The Vatican Council saw the proclamation of the Gospel as the first task of the priest.

> *'The people of God finds its unity through the word of the living God . . . since no one can be saved who has not first believed. Priests as co-workers with their bishops have, as their primary duty, the proclamation of Gospel of God to all . . . towards all people's priests have the duty of sharing Gospel truths . . . the gospel message draws all peoples to faith and the sacraments of salvation.'*

This passage makes it clear that sacramental ministry is to be found in the context of proclaiming the word. The eucharist is the completion or summit of the priest's work for the people.

The code of Canon Law continues the spirit of Vatican II.

> *'The parish priest is obliged to see to it that the word of God in its entirety is announced to those living in the parish . . . Christian faithful are instructed through the homily which is to be given on Sundays . . . he is to make every effort with the aid of the faithful to bring the Gospel message to those who have ceased practising their religion or who do not profess the true faith.'* (Canon 528 The Code of Canon Law *Collins, London 1983*).

The priest in proclaiming God's Word is doing this because like Christ he is called to do the Father's work, announcing the Kingdom. Vatican II stresses that the call to priesthood comes from the Father through Christ to the individual Christian.

> *'The priestly office shares in the authority by which Christ himself builds up, sanctifies and rules his body . . . priests are so configured to Christ that they act in the person of Christ the head.'* This is again echoed in the new *Code of Canon Law* which reflects the spirit of Vatican II. Canon 1008, speaking of the sacrament of orders, states: *'By divine institution some among Christ's faithful are through the sacrament of order constituted sacred ministers: thereby they are consecrated and deputed so*

that each according to his own grade they fulfil in the person of Christ the head, the offices of teaching, sanctifying and ruling so they nourish the people of God.'

However, despite the new vision of Vatican II, the exercise and understanding of priestly ministry in the Catholic tradition is the subject of much study and reflection. The American Catholic bishops have recently stated: 'Priestly ministry is not a finished reality, fully achieved, like a work of art. Neither is it something frail, a fragile object unable to withstand the taxing passage through change and time. Rather, what the sources of faith and theology reveal is a priestly ministry as a living reality, grounded securely through a threefold dynamic relationship. Its roots are in the mystery of the risen Lord and the Church. Its nature involves a mission of service to Christ and to the community. Its exercise occurs within the Church and its structures.'

In the light of this statement, I would like to look briefly at how I see the development of ministry, how our vision of the church and its origins influences such development, and finally to look at areas where growth of understanding is needed.

Among studies, from a Catholic viewpoint, on ministry and priesthood in the early Church, such works as *Ministry Traditions, Tensions and Transition* (23rd Publications, USA 1986) by William Bausch, *The Church with a Human Face* (SCM, London 1985) by Edward Schillebeeckx and *Priesthood* (Paulist Press, New York, 1988) by Kenan Osborne, provide comprehensive presentations of the subject. Fr Osborne's book is perhaps the best synthesis and evaluates more specialised studies. He makes the following points. Every study of church ministry must begin with a study of the ministry of Jesus which is the source and dynamism of all church ministry. As Jesus' ministry came from the Father then all church ministry must be a commissioning of the Lord. Jesus' ministry was one of love and service and this notion of *diakonia* is vital otherwise power structures can creep in. Jesus came to preach the kingdom and this must continue to be the message of Christian ministers. Belief in the resurrection is at the heart of the reality of the church and its service. This means that the risen Jesus continues his ministry in and through the church's ministry and therefore any study of church ministry is a study of the ministry of the Risen Lord.

The word 'church' raises the question when or how did Jesus found the church? The stance is now emerging that the church began with the Resurrection and belief in the Lordship of the Risen Christ. This means that while Jesus chose the 12 and gave his teachings to the 72 he did not impose a structure or form for all ages on his church — there was no blue print. Jesus left his intentions, his spirit, but gave the church total freedom to grow in the way that would best realize the kingdom. No, flexibility, taking responsibility would be the way of building the kingdom. Jesus lived for people, not for organizations, and so the church grew out of the people who lived and loved his message. This means that like the emergence of the New, Testament Canon, so the organizational structure of the church took a considerable time to be realized. Jesus called those close to him friends not slaves and in John 13 shows the style of ministry he envisaged, humble loving service. Today we realize that the vision of Jesus for ministry has been changed, expanded and diminished by political and cultural influences down the ages. Vatican II reminds us that the church has to be constantly renewing itself after the Spirit of the Gospel — the spirit of service.

What we see in the apostolic churches is a rich variety of ministries serving the wide range of needs of these new and vital communities. In Paul's communities, the apostle was the highest rank but after the apostle came the prophet and teacher. In other communities presbyters or elders emerged while elsewhere we have the '*episcopoi*' or overseers. These titles are it seems sometimes interchangeable but the titles do seem to stand for leadership in the local church. However what can seem puzzling to us is the fact that liturgical leadership is rarely mentioned. At this stage apostolic succession means one who witnesses to Jesus in a special way especially his Resurrection. The notion of apostolic succession is not a scriptural term and only appears in the second century to counter private revelation

116

of gnostics. One other interesting point is to recognize that the early church only used the word 'priest' for Jesus and for all the baptized.

The structure that is now held by the Catholic and Orthodox tradition of the head of the local church being called a bishop assisted by elders or presbyters' comes from the second century. It would seem that persecution and heresy caused the communities to fix on a pattern of monarchical leadership to ensure fidelity to the teaching handed on by the apostles. Ordination rituals such as those of Hippolytus appear but again it is noteworthy that pastoral leadership is the key function, liturgical leadership is not the focus of the rite.

However, the emergence of more centralized communities is the beginning of the hierarchical and clerical model of the Church. Ordination rather than baptism becomes the source of ministry and leads to jurisdictional power and status. The bishop with his elders or presbyters and deacons become the Church. Bernard Cooke in the *Distancing of God* (Fortress Press, Minneapolis 1990) sees a process of the Resurrection experience being gradually removed from the people. Bernard Botte, in his study *The Sacrament of Orders*, sees the church from Constantine onwards shaping itself after the pattern of the Roman Empire acquiring a juridical structure that tended towards the rigid. Here we have the beginning of an unresolved problem of how local bishops relate to the college of bishops and to the Pope. Getting the right balance will be a challenge which is still perhaps to be fully realized. What is more significant is the loss of awareness of the priesthood of all the baptized and of the vision that the Holy Spirit graces the community with various ministries. From now onwards the vision of ministry becomes that of priesthood founded on Aaron and focused on a cultic ritualistic model. Bausch makes the point that priesthood becomes defined as the power to celebrate the eucharist.

The Reformation and the Catholic response at the Council of Trent caused entrenchment of positions. The Reformers stressed the priesthood of all believers, the eucharist as a meal and also stressed proclaiming God's word, so the Catholic response was to emphasize the mass as a sacrifice and to point up the special nature of the ordained priest. However Trent did revitalize the moral and spiritual dimension of the Catholic priesthood and made a theological synthesis of medieval teaching. It did not, however, touch on Jesus' priestly ministry nor as a consequence did it see that the characteristics of Jesus' ministry as shown in the Gospel are the criteria of all Christian ministry. Rather the church and its power are defended. Another limitation is the focus on the eucharist as the centre of a theology of priesthood, preaching and leadership of the community are scarcely touched on. Finally, the role of bishop had come to be seen as an office and dignity in the church and not part of the sacrament of order. It almost seemed that the role of the bishop was one of privilege.

The Second Vatican Council holds a commanding place in Catholic teaching on the ministry. The documents of the Council and the new rituals for ordination mark a watershed and also offer a long term programme for renewal. Cardinal Marty offered the new vision in an address to a plenary session of the council,

> 'The Commission cannot agree with those Fathers who think the position paper should have followed the scholastic definition of priesthood, which is based on the power to consecrate the eucharist. According to the prevailing mind of this Council and the petition of many Fathers, the priesthood of presbyters must rather be connected with the priesthood of bishops, the latter being regarded as the high point and fullness of priesthood. The priesthood of presbyters must therefore be looked at, in this draft, as embracing not one function, but three, and must be linked with the Apostles and their mission.'

More important still was the Council's insistence on a Christological basis for ministry. Jesus is prophet/teacher – he proclaims the good news by his life.

> Jesus is priest – the one who brings holiness
> Jesus is leader – he is the shepherd who cares.

In the first place, the bishops carry out this work in the church as a college of bishops, and priests as collaborators of the bishops share in this same mission of Jesus which is given to his people — the church. This vision of ministry coming from Christ given to his church reactivates ministry among all the faithful because all are called in Christ and called to serve. The rise of lay ministry or collaborative ministry has been a marked feature of the life of the Catholic Church over the last 30 years. Pastoral care, teaching and sanctifying roles are now shared and readily accepted where good will allows such initiatives to flourish.

While Vatican II has rectified some imbalances in the understanding of priesthood there are still many issues to be clarified and developed.

The questions that still need to be explored begin with the need to work towards a clarification of the priestly ministry of Jesus himself. I would tend to follow a position adopted in the last century by Scheeben and expressed recently by the Catalan Carmelite theologian, Xiberta. Rather than see the emphasis put on the death of Jesus as the priestly sacrificial act, it would be more helpful to see the entire life, death and resurrection as the way Christ sanctifies us.

The relationship of the bishops and the papacy is still an area that needs clarification. We need to ask what are the limits of papal authority vis-à-vis the sacramental nature of episcopacy. In the years after the Council, the vision was Peter and the apostles, the Pope working with the apostles but a feeling is abroad that a centralizing spirit could obscure that vision.

A more practical question about the priesthood is the matter of celibacy. Pope Paul VI cut short discussion on this matter by calling it untimely. However, the issue is still with us and as a matter of church discipline it can be addressed in an appropriate forum. I personally believe celibacy is a precious grace in the church, but the question is, do all who wish to serve the church in the ordained ministry have to be endowed with this grace? I believe this question should be faced and a creative solution sought so that the work of building God's kingdom can be enabled.

Another area of development is an understanding of the relationship between the ordained and unordained ministry. The documents of the Council state the fact of a difference but there is no clear definition of the difference. The ministries that have emerged obviously flow from a call from Christ and are a consequence of our baptismal dignity. The challenge is to work out both the relationship and distinction between baptism and holy Orders. On the practical level it is a case of parish priests being open to the riches they can find in their communities. Certainly in areas of specialized ministry such as school, university and hospital chaplaincies, non-ordained Catholics are playing a vital role. Retreat ministry is another area where lay people are emerging in a 'teaching' role and enriching a vital aspect of church life.

The Roman Catholic priest today is by and large then a different person to his forebear of forty years ago. The isolation often brought on by the imposition of a quasi monastic spirituality has gone. Liturgical reforms mean that the worship he leads is more congregational and the deepening theological awareness of his congregation means that his teaching role is really that of a pastor. A priest working in the Highlands when asked to describe himself said he thought of himself as 'a holy man of God walking among his people'. A presence of leadership, called by God and a reminder of gospel values. This is a vision that is healthy and open.

Another aspect of changed perception is the fact that in England, a Catholic priest now works in collaboration with his colleagues in other churches. The work of ARCIC has enabled Catholics and Anglicans to respect each others ministries more deeply and the emphasis on the priest's teaching or prophetic role helps the Catholic value the Non-Conformist tradition. Again while the Catholic tradition situates the priest as a collaborator of his local bishop the emphasis on lay ministries brings a greater sympathy for a congregational model at the local level. Perhaps all the Christian traditions in this country have come to an awareness of the open and 'democratic' feel of the primitive Christian church. In the first Christian communities ministry was determined by the needs of that community and at the end of the twentieth century that is still a powerful criterion.

If the reader wishes to touch on the changing vision of ministry in the Catholic Church, a look at the novels of Graham Greene would be a good indicator. The whisky priest of *The Power and the Glory* is anxious above all to celebrate mass and goes to his doom because of his commitment to the sacraments. He is God's instrument, a channel of grace despite his unworthiness. In many ways he epitomizes the scholastic dictum that grace comes from sacraments despite the dispositions of the minister. Other of Greene's clergy in his early works speak of the awful mercy of God or are isolated by their calling. A gradual change comes so that in *The Burnt Out Case*, the mission superior is much more aware that he ministers in an ambiguous world. The priest in *The Honorary Consul* is inspired by Camilo Torres and echoes the earliest expressions of Liberation Theology. However in *Monsignor Quixote* we find a truly Christ-like figure who teaches from the simplicity of his friendship with Christ. Monsignor Quixote has a healthy disrespect for hierarchy but is able to reach his Marxist friend through his vision of God's mercy and his unwillingness to be dogmatic. As a critic commented, he incarnated the friendship of Christ.

One aspect of priesthood that is still unresolved is the question of women and the priesthood. This is not just an issue inside the Anglican communion, but one that has far reaching ecumenical consequences. The official position of the Catholic Church, from the statement of the Sacred Congregation for the Faith in 1976 down to the encounter between Dr Carey and Pope John Paul II in the Spring of 1992, is that Jesus intended to exclude women from priestly ministry for all times and under all sociological conditions. There is no apostolic tradition for the possible practice of ordaining women. This statement carries the weight of the formal authority of the Roman magisterium and has Papal approval. However the late Karl Rahner in an article 'Women and Priesthood' *Theological Investigations* Vol 20, 1981, would hold that the 1976 declaration is not a definitive decision and it is in principle reformable. Rahner argues that of course women were excluded by Jesus and the early church because of sociological factors. Equally so, the early church tolerated slavery. Discrimination against women and a low value of their worth was ingrained, but to accept that vision of women is not part of revelation. Rahner sees the exclusion of women as a human tradition that will change and become obsolete. The church once accepted slavery without question and now because of social and cultural change, opposes it.

Rahner hopes for a development on this question analogous to the change in the church's attitude on religious freedom. He concludes his article with the following respectful plea:

'The Roman Declaration says that in this question the Church must remain faithful to Jesus Christ. This is of course true in principle. But what fidelity means in connection with this problem remains an open question. Consequently the discussion must continue. Cautiously, with mutual respect, critical of bad arguments on both sides, critical of irrelevant emotionalism expressly or tacitly influencing both sides, but also with that courage for historical change which is part of the fidelity which the Church owes to its Lord.'

It is hoped that this development about ministry which has taken place in the reformed tradition will be resolved creatively. Certainly the question of women and ministry is an issue in the Catholic Church in some countries. Women are active in non-ordained ministries and look with deep interest at the position of their sisters elsewhere.

The Catholic Church has, then, been addressing the sacrament of orders with great energy. It has grown in understanding of the consequences of historical development and has expanded ministry while signalling the special position of bishop, priest and deacon. What is most important is that there is a firm vision that the teaching and example of Christ is the cornerstone for theory and practice as regards ministry. Christ is our safeguard against unproductive clericalism or a 'lay' secularization. Christ, the one who ministers by service, is the vision that any Christian minister must reproduce. The most poetic of the Pope's titles is Servant of the Servants of God and so if the centre of unity in the Roman Catholic Church service is the highest value in the service of the kingdom, so we hope it will be everywhere when communities live and worship. The ordained ministry for Catholics has to be a service of love so that at its peak, all may share in the highest outpouring of love, the eucharist. All of a Catholic priest's work is directed towards that action, the summit and peak of our Christian endeavour in this life.

8. Interpreters of the Word of God

A United Reformed Church perspective

Jack McKelvey

1. The One Ministry of the Whole People of God

The meaning of ordination depends upon the meaning of ministry and the meaning of the ordained ministry depends upon the meaning of the ministry given to the church. Jesus Christ, the crucified and risen Lord, dwells among God's people and his ministry becomes their ministry.

Thus the Manual of the U.R.C. begins by stating:

> *The Lord Jesus Christ continues his ministry in and through the Church, the whole people of God called and committed to his service and equipped by him for it (19).*

The ministry of all God's people may fairly be regarded as the modern equivalent of the so-called priesthood of all believers in the teaching of the Reformers and their followers. This doctrine was a counter-claim to what was deemed to be the Roman Catholic belief that access to God was through the ordained priest. The Reformers declared that every believer has the right to enter the presence of God and offer the sacrifice of praise and thanksgiving. Martin Luther, quoting 1 Pet 2.9, said 'because as priests we are worthy to appear before God and to pray for others and to teach one another the things of God'.[1] The same thought is to be found in the teaching of John Calvin:

> *Grant, Almighty God, that as you have made us a royal priesthood in your Son, we may daily offer to you spiritual sacrifice and be devoted to you both in body and soul.*[2]

In no sense therefore can the ordained ministry be regarded as a caste which exercises ministry independently of the ministry given to the church by its Lord. This is a necessary corrective on the one hand for the clericalism which continues to bedevil the churches and on the other hand for the narcissism that tends to enter into discussions on the ordained ministry.

In common with other churches, the U.R.C. regards baptism as the mode of entry into ministry:

> *We received the Spirit to equip us as members of Christ's body, the Church (Ordinal 1).*

Martin Luther, quoting the relevant New Testament passages, declared:

> *Through baptism all of us are consecrated as priests, as St.Peter says in 1 Peter 2.9, 'you are a royal priesthood, a priestly kingdom', and the Book of Revelation says (5.10), 'By your blood you made us to be priests and kings'.*[3]

The emphasis on baptism as the mode of entry into Christ's ministry has led to a discussion in the Reformed Churches on the question whether the term ordination and the practice of ordination to a particular ministry within the church should continue. There is also a belief for some that ordination implies a doctrine of 'orders' which is not part of the Reformed tradition. The Reformed Church in France has stopped using the word and speaks instead of 'recognition'. Fourteen forms of particular ministry are recognized by this church, including teachers of theology and administrative officers of districts. The U.R.C. does not believe that a full acceptance of the ministry of all the members of the church commits it to abandoning ordination to particular ministries.

Preparation of church members for ministry is a major concern in the U.R.C. The document *Patterns of Ministry in the U.R.C.* is before the churches for study and discussion in preparation for a major debate and action following the General Assembly 1992. Plans are in hand to identify and develop the particular knowledge, skills and attitudes necessary in ministry and to stimulate greater integration of training courses and personnel with a view to increasing the sense of partnership in ministry.

2. Particular Ministries

Within the total ministry of the church the Reformed churches make provision for particular ministries. Calvin did not interpret the New Testament woodenly and try to reproduce every ministry to be found there. Discussing the classic passage in Ephesians 4 (*Institutes* IV. iii. 4) he distinguished between ministries which had to do with the founding of the church in New Testament times ('the first builders of the Church', as he referred to them) and others which were ongoing. Included in the latter are pastors, teachers, elders and deacons. In the historical development of the Reformed churches the distinction between pastor and teacher has been a fluid one and is not nowadays maintained. P.T. Forsyth declared that 'the pastor is only the preacher in retail'.[4]

Similarly, in many churches today there is no separate office of deacons, diaconal aspects of ministry being undertaken by the elders.

Those aspects of the church's vocation which have been seen by the Reformed tradition as requiring permanent ministries are: proclamation of the Word of God and the administration of the sacraments, teaching and education, pastoral care, mission, diaconal service. Though each of these ministries has a distinct character they are not considered to be mutually exclusive and can be undertaken most effectively in a collegial partnership. In the U.R.C. they are the responsibility of two particular ministries: ministers of Word and Sacraments and elders. The collegial character of the ministry which is shared by minister and elders is emphasized by the fact that both minister and elders are ordained and by their sharing in the pastoral oversight and leadership of the local churches. They take counsel together in all the councils of the church, from local to national level.

The offices of the ministry of the Word and Sacraments and the eldership are open to both men and women and in the great majority of Reformed churches both men and women serve in these offices.

3. Ministries of Word and Sacraments

The great pre-supposition of the ministry of Word and Sacraments is the fact that Christianity is an historic faith. God has given the definitive revelation of himself in certain events of history. The significance of the witness to this revelation in every age needs to be interpreted. Hence the need of an office in the church for this purpose. In the Reformed tradition the primary function of the ordained minister is that of interpreting to the church the historic Word of God. This involves not only understanding the original records in the scriptures, but also what the churches have come to accept in the tradition, resulting from the interaction of the Word with the life of the people through the centuries.

Certain ancillary functions have attached themselves to this primary role, viz. liturgical, pastoral, and leadership. At this point the functions or the ordained ministry begin to merge with those of the elders.

In a day and age when the ministry of all Christians is emphasized to the point at which ordination is in danger of

127

being demoted it is necessary to affirm the distinctiveness of the ordained ministry. The job of the ordained ministry is not doing what other members of the church might do if they had the time. Nor is it simply equipping members of the church for their ministry. It is pre-eminently to interpret the distinctive, historic Word of God which makes and keeps the church Christian.

In ordaining a person to the ministry of the Word and Sacraments the church is saying to him/her: study the Word of God, discover what it is saying to us and then bring what you find to us, without fear or favour, and we will listen to your message for this matters to us more than everything else. It is here that the minister's authority lies. As he/she is seen to be scrupulously responsible to the Word of the Gospel, i.e. under its authority, the minister's message will be respected and accepted, however unpalatable. The distinctiveness of the ministry of the Word and Sacraments was given classical expression by Bernard Lord Manning:

> *You are not to consider yourselves as delegating to him, because you judge him likely to be reasonably competent, certain duties which (if you were not such busy and important people) you ought in truth to do for the Saviour yourselves . . . In one way it is true that our brother is to be your minister, but in a far deeper and more important way he is a minister of the Word and the Sacraments, a minister of the Gospel, a minister of Christ. From the Word that he preaches, from the Sacraments that he administers, from the Gospel that he sets forth, from Christ Whom he serves – from these first and most, from you in only a secondary way – he derives the power and the function and the grace with which we pray today that his ministry is to be marked . . . The things that make a man a good minister of Jesus Christ come from God most high: you can neither bestow them nor take them away. The weakness or the strength, the coldness or the devotion of the Church that ordains, as you ordain tonight, affect not in the least the validity*

or the fulness of the august commission that a minister receives. At your hands indeed he receives the commission; but it is Christ's commission, not yours; and it comes from Christ, not you. When your minister speaks, mark whose word it is that he speaks. You do not hear from him an echo of your own voice. It is the Word of God that he proclaims, no word that you have committed to him tonight. The minister is not the creation of the Church. The Church is sometimes his creation.[5]

Basic to ordination in the Reformed tradition is the call of God. In declaring that 'some (of its members) are called to the ministry of Word and Sacrament . . . some are called to be elders', the U.R.C. is giving expression to one of the oldest and most universally-held tenets of Reformed teaching. Thus Calvin declared, 'if anyone would be considered a true minister of the Church, he must first have been duly called' (*Inst* iv. iii. 10). Calvin made a distinction between an 'inner' and an 'outer' call. The 'inner' or 'secret' call, as he sometimes described it, is the call 'of which each minister is conscious before God, and which does not have the Church as witness' (*Inst*. iv. iii. 11). The outer call 'has to do with the public order of the Church' (*ibid*). Nowadays the candidate's call is tested at local, provincial and national levels for fitness of character, Christian commitment, service in the Church, and educational qualifications. The candidate is expected to undertake a prescribed course of theological education and training. On its successful completion he/she is introduced to a church and if the church believes that this is the person who should be its minister a call is then issued. The call must have the concurrence of the District Council before it is issued. This is the church's authentication of the individual's own call.

An illustration of the fundamental importance of the call which is sometimes cited in Reformed circles is the case of Robert Bruce. A theologically-qualified layman (lecturer in theology), Bruce was worshipping in his church in Edinburgh in 1987 on a communion Sunday when for some reason the minister was not present. The congregation asked Bruce to administer the Sacrament, to which he agreed. Bruce regarded this call to serve the church as his ordination to the ministry and it was recognised by the presbytery. Bruce went on to exercise an influential ministry, twice officiating as Moderator of the General Assembly.

It can be said that in the Reformed tradition the *sine qua non* of admission to ministerial office is the call (understood in the two above-mentioned senses), though this is invariably followed by the formal act of ordination. The emphasis on the call in the Reformed tradition is part and parcel of the belief that ministry is a gift of God to his church. It points to the fact that the ministry of Word and Sacraments is understood to arise not out of the church, in the sense of the church being able to confer certain specific powers on individuals to perform certain functions, but is a charisma or gift of God to his people. The church has the responsibility of recognizing the call, equipping the ordinand by education, training and Christian nurture, and finally authorizing him/her on the satisfactory completion of the process of screening, education and training as a person considered to be fit for ministry.

4. Elders

The ordination of elders and the ministry which they exercise is characteristic of Reformed churches and has been accepted by other Protestant churches. The ministers of Word and Sacraments do not function on their own. Serving along with them and sharing in the pastoral oversight and leadership of the church is a team of elders. John Calvin considered eldership to be indispensable.

*Now experience itself makes clear that this sort of order was not confined to one age . . . it is necessary for all ages (*Inst. *IV. 3, 8).*

Thus in Reformed churches minister and elders form the executive body which is found in other churches. The difference

130

in the Reformed churches is that its members are all ordained. Their ordination implies that the office of elder is not an *ad hoc* arrangement convened to deal with some temporary need in the church, but is a permanent office.

A fresh study of eldership was undertaken by the Reformed churches in response to an enquiry by the World Council of Churches on the document *Baptism, Eucharist and Ministry* (1982).[6] This showed that while the Reformed churches regard eldership as a self-evident requirement for the churches' life and ministry and one of the great strengths of the Reformed churches, practice varies in the selection, ordination, term of service, and training of elders. An attempt has been made to share thinking and consult with one another. They have also accepted the ecumenical responsibility to help churches in other traditions to understand what it is in the office of elder which is regarded as crucial to the life and mission of the Church.

In the U.R.C. elders share with the minister the responsibility *inter alia* of pastoral care of the congregation and ensuring that public worship is regularly offered and the sacraments administered, the oversight of work among children and young people and of all organisations within the congregation and the maintenance of church property, and the oversight of the finances. Elders elected by the Church Meeting (of members) are ordained and inducted by the minister to serve for such periods as are determined by the Church Meeting. All elders are eligible for election and those re-elected are inducted for a further term of service. Elders who move to a different locality and church are eligible for election by that church and, if elected, are inducted. They are not re-ordained. In other words, the elder like the minister, is primarily an elder of the church and not just of the local church.

Training is available for elders and prospective elders are strongly encouraged to undertake this training.

In situations where a congregation does not have a minister or interim-minister the congregation sometimes empowers one of the elders to act as presiding elder or moderator and to administer the sacraments. A proposal is before the U.R.C. which would empower each local church to appoint a presiding elder who would be authorized to preside at the sacrament of the Lord's Supper. The intention is to provide every local church with regular sacramental worship.

The Act of Ordination

The service of ordination is normally held in the congregation to which the ordinand is inducted. The wider church is represented by members of the District Council and the Moderator of the Synod who presides. The local church shares in this service. Its members are asked to affirm their faith and promise to pray for and support the minister. The ordination of elders also takes place in the church in which they are to serve, but no representatives of the wider church are required to be present.

'In ordination the two things must meet − the man's (sic) call (not by religious sensitivity *but by the gospel*) and the church's seal of it − the authority of the Spirit in the man; and the recognition of it by the church. There is the creative and sacramental authority, and there is the judicial and licensing authority.'[7]

Although it is invariably the experience of the great majority of those who are ordained into the Reformed ministry that the act of ordination reinforces their sense of call, strengthens their resolution, and gives them a profound sense of the sacredness of their calling, the Reformed tradition does not hold that ordination conveys a special grace or 'character'. Much of the difficulty which Reformed Christians, in common with others of different traditions, have experienced in regard to ordination, especially in regard to the laying on of hands and questions like 'what happens in ordination?' or 'does ordination make a difference?', result from our looking at the act of ordination in isolation from all that has gone before or all that still has to take place. Misunderstanding and confusion will be avoided if we view ordination as the act whereby the church formally recognizes the ordinand's calling by God and the spiritual gifts and attitudes for ministry which have already

132

been conferred by God and thereby sets him/her apart for this task. Ordination is authorization. In setting this particular individual apart with prayer the church is authorizing him/her to use his/her gifts for the good of the church and its mission. Thus in the U.R.C. service of ordination God is asked to:

Strengthen the gifts you have given him/her that the ministry and mission of your people may bear fruit.

This is all of a piece with what has been said above in regard to the total ministry exercised by the church.

The Reformed tradition has always been anxious to make it clear that the laying on of hands does not mean conferring upon the candidate something which he/she did not already possess but is to be understood as a consecration, setting the person apart for a solemn and life-long vocation. Some early orders like the *Ordonnances ecclesiastiques of Geneva* (1541) deliberately omitted the laying on of hands on the grounds that it might be taken to convey the conferring of power (*potestas*) as in the ordination of a Roman Catholic priest. Calvin did not however dissaprove of the rite (*Inst.* IV. iii. 16). In Scotland the imposition of hands was not alas used in the beginning. John Knox did not have hands laid upon him. The same is true of others like Andrew Melville and Robert Bruce. Indeed the term ordination was also avoided to begin with, though in the *Second Book of Discipline* (1878) it is used along with the laying on of hands. In course of time the imposition of hands for the ordination of both ministers and elders became virtually standard practice in the Reformed churches.[7]

Although the act of ordination is not thought of as conferring a sacramental character (the so-called 'indelible character') upon the candidate, which would make him or her different from other Christians, a number of things in the Reformed tradition cause the question to be asked: Does ordination give a certain indelible status?[8] For one thing, ordination is for life. In 17th century Scotland and France it was laid down that anyone who vacated pastoral charge for some other occupation should be excommunicated. Such persons were called deserters. Furthermore, the principle of no re-ordination was established from the beginning. Priests who left the Catholic church to join the Reformed church and Reformed ministers who elected to serve the Church of England after the Restoration in 1660 were not re-ordained. All this goes to show that although the Reformed churches rejected any idea of an 'indelible' character they did think of an inalienable office or life-long responsibility. This applies equally to elders. The expectation is that ordination is for life. The only real way of defrocking a minister or elder is by disciplining him or her for action in a way unworthy of the gospel.

There is no significant difference in the act of ordination of ministers and of elders in the U.R.C. For both it is a solemn setting-apart and authorization. The difference lies not in the ordination itself but in the office to which they are ordained. The minister, in addition to the responsibilities of the elder, has also got the task of keeping the church loyal to its foundation Jesus Christ by preaching and teaching the word of the gospel and by the administration of the sacraments. It is the job that is different, not the mode of entry into it.

Who ordains? It is God acting through his servants. He gives the charism; the church authorizes to office. The Reformers in doing away with the order of bishop were hesitant about prescribing a substitute. The result was that various practices arose, which depended in some cases on the availability of ministers since in the early years of the Reformed movement not all churches had ministers and some had to act in vacant churches as Superintendents.

What was agreed upon quite early was that ordination of ministers should not be the sole responsibility of any local church. The local church should play a part but the responsibility for arranging an ordination should lie with the church at large. In the U.R.C. it is the District Council which exercises this responsibility. The point which the church has been anxious to convey is that the ministry belongs to the whole church.

Included in the ordination service is the induction. Whereas ordination is the mode of entry into the church at large and is not repeated, induction is to service in the local church and is repeated whenever a minister or elder is called to serve in a different local church. In the case of both ministers and elders induction is authorization to serve in the congregation in question, the renewal of promises, and the prayer for God's help in the new ministry just beginning.

Conclusion

John Calvin's statement that:

> *(Christ) alone should rule and reign in the Church as well as have authority or pre-eminence in it and this authority should be exercised and administered by his Word alone (Inst.* iii.1)

more than anything else perhaps points to the Reformed understanding of ministry and ordination. Ministers of the Word and Sacraments are, above all, called and ordained to be interpreters of the Word of God. The Word is God's gift and with it the ministry. The charisms necessary to undertake ministry are conferred by God and God alone. Thus the church does not create its ministry. It recognizes it and authorizes it.

The point at which the gifts necessary for ministry are given to an individual or when these gifts become discernible is beyond human knowing. They can be given and become discernible at different times and at different stages. Certainly they will have been given and will have been in evidence before the day of ordination, when they will, under God, be acknowledged by the church.

The U.R.C. does not claim that its particular offices of minister of Word and Sacraments and elder are the definitive expression of New Testament church order. It acknowledges that there were other forms of ministry in New Testament times. This means that the U.R.C. is open to the possibility of discovering in ecumenical dialogue forms of ministry which are different from what it has today. The Scheme of Union of the U.R.C. states:

> *The United Reformed Church shall determine from time to time what other ministries may be required and which of them should be recognised as ministries of the whole Church.*

A similar openness was characteristic of John Calvin. He clearly showed that the church needs ministry in order to fulfil its vocation, but when he came to describe particular ministries he showed remarkable caution. He acknowledged the multiplicity of offices in Ephesians 4 and made distinction between them. While he could not think of the church without ministers of the Word and Sacraments he did think of its doing without some of the ministries listed in Ephesians 4. In his reflections on deacons he used words like 'unless my judgement deceives me' (*Inst. IV*. iii. 9). When he said, in regard to elders, that 'experience itself makes clear that this sort of order was not confined to one age' (*IV*. iii. 9) it is pragmatism, not scriptural warrant, which guided the Reformer. Calvin clearly left the door open for future insights and developments. The U.R.C. believes that openness is essential in interpreting the New Testament and the Christian tradition concerning ministry.

Notes

1. *Christian Liberty* ii 338. cf *Address to the Nobility*, 2.66.
2. Commentary on Malachi 2.9; *Institutes* II.15.6; cf R.S. Wallace, *Calvin's Doctrine of the Christian Life* Oliver and Boyd, Edinburgh 1959, 28f.
3. *Address to the Nobility* ii.66.
4. *The Church and the Sacraments*, Independent Press, London, 1917, 145.
5. *A layman in the Ministry*, Independent Press, London 1942. 152, 153.
6. *Eldership in the Reformed Churches today*, ed, Lukas Vischer, Geneva 1991.
7. P.T. Forsyth, *op cit*. p. 138.
8. J.L. Ainslie, *The Doctrines of the Ministerial Order in the Reformed Churches*, T. & T. Clark, Edinburgh 1940, 157ff.
9. Ainslie, *op cit*, pp. 194ff.

9. Called, Gifted and Authorized

An Anglican woman's perspective

Vera Sinton

An ordination service is a rite of passage. When I was ordained there was a flurry of activity with relatives arranging accommodation, transport and food. Friends from many phases of my life dressed as for a wedding and arrived in time to find a good seat in one of England's ancient and awesome cathedrals. Believers rubbed shoulders with slightly nervous unbelievers as they studied an unfamiliar service sheet and watched warily to see if they should stand or sit. All understood that this impressive ceremony publicly marked me out for a lifetime of work in the Christian church.

Beyond that it is impossible to know how my various guests understood the service. The music, the children, the architecture, the liturgical language or lack of visibility in a big nave – any of these could have distracted attention at the crucial time. But to the fairly intelligent visitor, who was able to hear and digest the words, the central action of the service was clearly highlighted. Someone already ordained, with an authoritative role in the church, laid hands on my head and called to God.

*'Send down the Holy Spirit
upon your servant Vera
for the office and work
of a deacon in your Church.'*

There is an important tension in that prayer. It acknowledges that the authority and ability to serve and to lead in the church of Jesus Christ is a gift of God's grace. It comes from his initiative by the Holy Spirit, the power and presence of the Eternal God in us and among us. But how are others to recognize that the gift has been given? Visible signs like flames or doves or audible voices rarely occur in our generation. Deciding who God has appointed requires a mixture of faith and judgement. The overseer who officiates at an ordination represents the combined resources of the church that has made that judgement.

A chain of touch from one set of hands to another going backwards and forwards through history links me physically with nearly everyone else who has ever been ordained in the Christian church. There have been times when the needs of mission or the pain of division have caused breaks in the chain but it remains a powerful symbol of the geographical and historical continuity of the church. The decision to recognize me publicly as someone ordained by God to minister in Christ's church was taken in a 'collegial' way by a variety of people who are aware of my gifts, the needs of the local and national church. At least some had knowledge of the international and historical dimensions of the church. I recall one visitor from another denomination commenting to me, 'It sounded as if it was something more than just the Anglican Church you were being ordained into.'

Questions about ordination that constantly have to be addressed in a theological college are:

What is unique about ordained ministry?
How do we discern that this is God's appointment?
Who may be ordained? (A woman, for instance?)

In this chapter I will briefly explore these issues but first, to put them in perspective, I will examine concepts of ministry in the Bible, looking particularly at three Old Testament roles and three New Testament themes.

Ministry in the Old Testament – Three Roles

Three specific roles or offices of ministry dominate the Old Testament story and permeate the thinking of New Testament writers, namely the roles of Prophet, Priest and Shepherd or King. Notice, for instance, in the Exodus period how the leadership of the newly rescued Israel is in the hands of a family trio occupying the three roles.

Miriam is a prophet. It is clear from Num 11 & 12 that this involves direct activity of the Holy Spirit. The Lord puts his Spirit on a prophet (11.25,29) and that person is a direct mouthpiece for the Lord (12.1). Little detail is given about Miriam's ministry. The main incident where she is seen in action is at the moment of celebration after the rescue from Egypt (Ex 15.21). Miriam leads a song and dance which interprets the experience the people have just come through and turns it into doxology (glorifying God) which is what all good theology (speaking of God) is about.

Aaron is also described as a prophet but he soon becomes the founder member of Israel's priesthood. If the emphasis in prophecy is on the unpredictable and overwhelming initiative of the Spirit, with priesthood there is a clear and exclusive tradition to determine who is to be called priest. A male descendant of Aaron without any major disease or physical blemish at the prescribed age is admitted. All others, however worthy are excluded. One of the examples of the evil of Jereboam as he tried to establish the northern kingdom after Solomon is presented with these words, 'Anyone who wanted to become priest, he consecrated.' (1 Kings 13.33) The ritual of ordination in Lev 8 is elaborately detailed. It is a visual way of teaching that the Lord is both glorious and staggeringly awesome in his holiness. Nothing that defiles or destroys has any place in his presence. But sinfulness with all its destructive effects is deep-rooted in human society and human hearts. Those whose task is to help others approach a holy God for reconciliation on the basis of sacrifice must first be thoroughly cleansed themselves.

No one title is assigned to Moses throughout the Pentateuch. Like the others he is described as a prophet; in Deut 18.18 he is a model for all future prophets. At the ordination of Aaron he acts as the consecrating priest. But supremely he is the unique leader of God's people, a national saviour. When Moses eventually looks for a successor he looks for a shepherd, someone who will lead the people in and out (Num 27.17). The Lord is leading the journey through the wilderness and Moses is his human agent. They speak face to face as a man speaks to his friend (Ex 33.11).

There is a conflict within the Old Testament as to whether the covenant people of God need a systematically appointed supreme leader. The Lord himself is the true shepherd of the flock. What kind of undershepherds are required? Moses, Gideon, Nehemiah respond like prophets to a personal divine call and take responsibility in the moment of crisis or need. Joshua, Saul and David are appointed by a predecessor or a prophet. The advantages and disadvantages of hereditary kingship are thrashed out but eventually the succession of Davidic kings is reckoned to be God's plan despite the failures and abuses. This method of appointment is more like the priestly than the prophetic and the two roles support each other in authority. Priests anoint kings. Kings protect or reform the priesthood. The experience of Joash in 2 Kings 11 & 12 exemplifies the relationship.

The divine appointment of prophet, priest and shepherd in the Old Testament is not incompatible with severe failure of the people appointed. Miriam, Aaron and Moses are all shown in serious and sinful failure which is potentially damaging for their leadership. Miriam takes the lead in criticism of Moses, probably tinged with envy, which might undermine his leadership at a delicate stage of the journey (Num 12). Aaron fails to withstand the pressure of the crowd in Moses' absence and makes a golden calf (Ex 32). Moses loses his temper and fails to trust and honour God in the exercise of miraculous power (Num 20). Real damage is done and there is a personal cost in these failures but the incidents serve to underline the forgiving mercy of a God who redeems sinners and commissions them to serve him. Being weak or having sinned does not disqualify a person from ministry.

Like Moses some of the other Old Testament giants combine all three roles. Abraham the patriarchal leader who received a prophetic call acts as a priest when he sacrifices a ram on Mount Moriah. King David's sacrifice on the threshing floor of Araunah defines the site for the temple he planned. His psalms include the key prophetic texts from which Jesus and the apostles argued our Lord's Messiahship. The prophet Elijah single-handedly rallies the believers as he takes on the priests of Baal. Among Old Testament women Deborah in Judg 4 & 5 is a prophet and the nation's supreme leader in her day. There is no sacrificial ritual in her story but blessing (and its converse, cursing) occupies an important place in her victory song.

Ministry in the New Testament – Three Vital Emphases

There is a gap of two and a half millennia between an Anglican cathedral ordination today and the time when prophets rubbed shoulders with priests and kings in ancient Israel. But the connection for the Christian church is abiding because the apostolic writers of the New Testament described the ministry of Jesus Christ in language which deliberately emphasizes how he fulfils the three roles. Understanding them has been vital for understanding the gospels and they have moulded the development of Christian ministry roles. At the same time we have to be honest and note that each age has had a biased understanding and has tended to interpret them in ways that suit the culture and concerns of the current generation. I acknowledge that in what follows the reader will identify some of my own bias and concerns.

Three things stand out for me in the New Testament as key emphases of Christian ministry and each of them has some expression in the prophetic, the priestly and the pastoral leadership roles.

1. Teaching The first is teaching in its widest sense including proclamation or preaching. Prophets received the word of God and passed on truth which was rational, pictorial and passionate. They argued, they told parables and wrote poems, they acted out dramas and used visual aids, they rehearsed familiar phrases from the law and the covenant. Their particular emphasis was the immediate challenge and appeal, a specific word for the day. Even when they talked about the future it was to encourage faith, commitment or reformation in the present.

Priests teach the law was Jeremiah's summary to distinguish priests from prophets or from sages (Jer 18.18). The liturgical rites of sacrifices and of festivals taught through the experience of five senses. The daily, weekly or annual repetitions emphasized unchanging truths about the nature of God. This kind of teaching required a trained institutional priesthood which passed on its tradition carefully. But it was not an esoteric tradition. In post-exilic Jerusalem at the festivals of renewal, Ezra the priest and his assistants read the Book of the Law of God to men, women and children capable of understanding. They explained it so that everyone understood what was being read (Neh 8.3,8).

Leaders and kings were also in a sense national teachers. The great prayers and exhortations before major events, battles or building projects, rehearsed the foundation of Israel's faith, God's character, his covenant, his past actions and his future promises. It was on these that the authority of the godly leader was based, the power of the word of God to unite his people as a flock and to move them forward together. This is theocratic power which is also democratic in the sense that the people constantly exercise the responsibility of choice. 'Choose for yourselves this day whom you will serve.' (Josh 24.15) The anxieties about kingship centred round the likelihood that in a fallen world the king will substitute for the authority of God's word a weighty bureaucracy, a mighty armed force or compromising political alliances.

Significant voices today are emphasizing teaching as the dominant model with which to interpret ordained ministry. I am excited and encouraged by that so long as the full range and variety of biblical examples is allowed to inform our concept of what constitutes teaching and how the people of God learn. Serious distortions arise if the definition is too narrow, however. Expository sermons are an excellent and vitamin rich staple for a congregation but they do not cover the full range of its dietary needs.

2. Discipline Christian ministry has an important component of discrimination. It involves making judgements about what is good and genuine. The servant of Christ shares the master's passionate commitment for all that is consistent with the loving holiness of God and against all which defiles and destroys. John's gospel shows us how the words and actions of Jesus required people to make a choice between light and darkness. They produced in the present the crisis or judgement which has its ultimate and eternal form in the future (Jn 3.19, 5.24.).

The three Old Testament roles illuminate the disciplinary aspects of ministry. Prophets denounced specific and general instances of economic oppression, violence or sexual disorder. They particularly stressed the connection between such sin and the worship of false images. (The emphasis is still highly relevant today though the idols have mainly become fast-moving media images.) Priests operated the sacrificial system which led sinners into forgiveness and fellowship with the living God without overlooking the seriousness of sin.

The rational leaders were often involved in rooting out sin, orchestrating times of repentance, helping the people experience the forgiving grace of God. But leaders were also involved in discipline of a different order. Their task included restricting the freedom and scope of individuals in the interests of activities and projects which require team work and benefit people collectively.

We tend to make a distinction between issues of moral and spiritual principle and practical matters to do with our relationships and interdependence within the church. In fact the distinction is not always easy to operate. Questions about leadership and ordained ministry often lie on the borderline. Should presiding at the eucharist be a function reserved for those ordained priest or presbyter? For some the answer is a resounding 'yes' grounded in spiritual principle. They believe that this order of ministry was ordained by Christ. God in his grace allows the believer's experience of the presence of Christ in the sacrament to be mysteriously linked with the priest as representative of Christ. Others deny that principle and allow lay people to preside when it seems convenient and practical; they may encourage lay presidency as a vigorous demonstration of a different theology of the communion. A third approach does not believe that the effectiveness of the eucharist hinges on an ordained president but considers that the long-standing Christian tradition about this is an important way of upholding other fundamental principles. An Anglican like myself may hold that the unity of the universal church of Christ is intended to have visible expression and that the tradition which down the centuries maintained mutual recognition and intercommunion between Christian congregations needs to be taken very seriously.

I worked a few years ago in an interdenominational context where communion was regularly celebrated in a variety of different rites and styles. The community contained women who were in leadership roles and women who were training for ministry. In general it was very affirming to their ministry, but without bringing the matter to open discussion, the leaders drew a line against women presiding in the communion. They judged it would cause offence to the minority who held that an important theological principle was at stake. There was no hesitation, however, in allowing a lay man to preside despite the fact that a similar sized minority came from churches where that would have been an offence.

Obviously in that community the debate about gender in ministry was evoking much stronger feelings than the issue of lay versus ordained. The disciplinary role of the Christian leader in this kind of situation involves tracing a path from biblical revelation, through theological principles, into the realities of the present day situation and reaching a decision that commands respect for its justice and coherence. Strong feelings are a reality which have to be taken into account on the way but in the end they must not have the last word. Feelings change as respect and commitment grow around a communal decision.

3. Nurturing care A third vital ingredient of New Testament ministry is face to face relationships of love which respect and nurture the growth of the individual and provide compassionate care in situations of need and pain. The gospel writers may emphasize Jesus as a great teacher of the crowds, portraying him strong in the conflict with forces of darkness and opposition, but they also devote many column inches to detailed accounts of his healing encounters in the lives of individuals. 'We loved you so much,' wrote Paul to the Thessalonians 'that we were delighted to share with you not only the gospel of God but our lives as well, because you had become so dear to us'(1 Thess 2.8).

Tracing this theme in the ministry of prophet and priest I will leave to the reader. Let me linger on leader or king. It is precisely here that the metaphor of shepherd becomes so important. It is used at many points in the Old Testament but gets its fullest exposure in Ezek 34. There the Lord himself is the ideal shepherd for his people but there is also a promise of a Davidic king who will fulfil the role. The chapter brings out the range of activities involved in tending a flock. Sheep need to move as a flock from one place to another with a shepherd to give direction and keep them together. Sheep need protection from outside dangers and sometimes from other aggressive sheep. On the pasture they need space and freedom to graze individually choosing their own patch but without getting too far apart from the flock. When they are sick or weak or wounded they need individual care.

I deliberately avoided using for this section the heading pastoral care. We have been through a period when that term has been used in the church to focus almost exclusively on individual care for the weak and hurting. This has passed over into the secular world and 'pastoral studies' has begun to appear on curricula covering the concerns of the caring professions. Meanwhile in the last decade within the church pastoral theology has taken a closer look at the biblical roots of the concept of pastoring. The result has been two-fold. On the one hand we are more positive about the debt we owe to generations of twentieth century therapists. Not only have they spent long hours giving care and hope to needy individuals but they have also worked hard to find frameworks in which they can pass on systematically to others what they have learnt about the human mind and emotions. On the other hand we are less defensive about the fact that a Christian minister will not normally be a psychotherapist, as a shepherd is not normally a vet. Pastor is a very comprehensive word indicating a well balanced concern with the mission and ministry of Christ's Church.

What is Unique About Ordained Ministry?

So far I have been examining the concept of Christian ministry by laying it out on a 3 x 3 grid with the role models of prophet, priest and pastor on one axis and the functions of teaching, discipline and care on the other. Now comes the crucial question for a book or ordination: what part of the chart is exclusive to ordained ministry?

To that question, my reply is 'Nothing'. There is a succinct phrase which is the title of a Church of England report, *All Are Called* (Church House Publishing, London 1986). Every Christian believer who affirms faith in the Father who created the world, the Son who redeemed it and the life-giving Spirit and who turns to Christ, repenting of sin, renouncing evil, is by baptism a publicly accredited minister of Jesus Christ and his gospel.

As all the Old Testament models and roles of ministry come together and are 'fulfilled', in the sense of finding their full expression in Jesus Christ, so at Pentecost they become the model for the ministry of every disciple. The old boundary lines which divided and hindered mutual fellowship and ministry are gone. Paul singles out in Gal 3.28 the divisions of religion and culture (Jew and Greek), socio-economic divisions (slave and free) and the gender divide (male and female). These do not disappear from the world but their restricting power is ever undermined by the gospel. Included in the good news is the truth that every individual Christian is firstly a son or daughter loved and affirmed in God's family on the model of Jesus the Unique Son and secondly sent out on the Father's business as was Jesus the Servant of God.

So Christian laity are potentially priests, intended to lead one another in worship, to intercede for others, to bring others into contact with the living God though the reconciling sacrifice of Jesus. They are holy people whose lives more and more reflect the light of God as they spend time in his presence.

Christian laity are potentially prophets. It is the privilege of all believers to have access to the Word of God and to the Spirit of God who brings into their minds truths and insights from God applying to the modern situation and compatible with his revealed character and will. The apostle Paul urged the Corinthian believers to be eagerly desiring the verbal prophetic gifts.

All of us, including the deprived and damaged, have some sphere of influence over others where we teach, confront and care. All Christians are called by the master shepherd to feed his sheep and sometimes we are amazed when we discover the scope of that. When we feel most helpless and in need of others we may find we are teaching and building up those who ostensibly are caring for us. Christ's ministry was exercised with great power in those final hours of pain and torture on the cross.

I have heard many attempts to define an element of Christian ministry which is exclusively for the ordained and each of them seems to leave the gifts of many lay people denied or undervalued. All Christian ministry belongs to the baptized. What about different gifts, however? All are called to the one ministry of the Church, the body of Christ but each of us has a different combination of the qualities and abilities which are required for that ministry and this is seen as a positive and important fact in the Christian faith. The Spirit of God gives us different gifts by his grace. It is God's will that we all play distinct and unique parts in the whole drama. Surely we can at least define the minimum qualifications in terms of essential gifts?

Once again this turns out to be dangerous ground. I have spent twenty years in Christian ministry, most of it with a strong focus on training Christian leaders. Each time I feel I have a clear conception of essential qualities, I have had to tear up the list and start again. The examples in scripture and church history confirm my experience in the modern world — God has an endless ability to surprise us with the unlikely characters he uses to serve him and lead others. It is almost as if the heavenly composer says, 'I am a bit bored with violin concertos, good though they are. Let's write one for the kettle drum today.'

Perhaps, however, there is a clue in that metaphor. There is a great variety of instruments in the orchestra and any one of them could take the lead but it has got to be in tune with the others and committed to the composer's purpose, willing to play the tune. The ordained minister is a representative of the ministry of the body of Christ. Lots of my theological bedfellows shudder at that word because of some of the nuances it has been given, but I cannot find a more accurate metaphor than the idea of a group of people accepting one of their number to be a good example of the kind of people they are, to have an understanding of their range and diversity and to be a good communicator of their common goals.

In the theological college where I teach we have analysed our goals for training ordained ministers into three categories. The first assumes that the minister should be a good example of a Christian, grounded and growing in prayer and Christian character. The second assumes that ministers should be discovering and developing their unique set of gifts for ministry and seeing how they fit alongside the gifts of others. The third goal assumes they should have a good foundation in knowledge and understanding of the biblical revelation and of Christian thought and worship down the centuries and be able to relate it to mission and ministry in specific contexts in the modern world.

Becoming an acknowledged representative puts a person in the limelight. Anyone who is a focus of attention is likely to become a role model for others and has an increased opportunity to communicate aims and goals to others. It is notable that the prescriptions for bishops and deacons in 1 Tim 3 are mainly boundary lines to ensure that they command the respect of outsiders and are good examples for those within the church. Two phrases are of a different order. Bishops should be 'apt to teach' (v 2) and deacons should 'keep hold of the deep truths of the faith' (v 9). Ordained ministers should be good examples and good communicators of what Christian disciples (in all their diversity) are intended to be.

How Should the Ordained be Selected?

We have already noted briefly the contrast in the Old Testament between the prophetic call which comes unexpectedly to the individual often in dramatic circumstances and the public anointing of priests which follows a predictable tradition. In the New Testament Paul describes himself as called to be an apostle (Rom 1.1) and Acts gives us three accounts of his call with the specific ministry of taking the gospel to the Gentiles featuring in each version. The gospels each tell of Jesus calling specific disciples to follow him at the start of his ministry.

Down the centuries the church has tended to make the prophet's call the paradigm for a 'vocation' to ordained ministry and for other full time ministries such as missionary or nun. In the process it has often lost sight of the way in which the apostolic writers understood the significance of 'call' for Christians. A study of the language of call in the New Testament reveals that the Old Testament prophetic call is now being applied to the experience of every believer at conversion.

149

Christians in all walks of life have been called by God at conversion to serve and follow Jesus whatever their level of personal freedom in society. That is why some verses about slavery slip into the middle of Paul's discussion of marriage in 1 Corinthians 7.[1] Slaves and wives remained subordinate members of the household hierarchy in the Roman empire but they have a new status in the gospel: called to follow Jesus.

The report *Call to Order* (ACCM Church House, London 1989) on Vocation and Ministry in the Church of England suggested that we should try and return to language which clearly distinguishes a three-fold process:

1. All are called to discipleship and service. This is where vocation language should be used.
2. All are gifted by the Spirit but with different gifts for a variety of service.
3. Some are appointed to authorized ministry roles, particularly the ordained.

What is the practical issue at stake in this linguistic change? It is not a denial that individuals have strong spiritual experiences in which they feel that God has guided them towards ordained ministry and which sustain them as they steer their way through the selection process. It is denying that an experience of such a specific call is a necessary condition. All candidates need to have the basic conviction of a vocation to discipleship and service. For some the decision to be ordained will be experienced as a response to others who seek them out and affirm how their gifts match the needs of the church.

Anglicans usually expect a candidate first to 'have a vocation' and then to 'test a vocation'. This assumes the initiatives come from a candidate and the role of others is passive and critical. In practice well established culture groups in the church have discrete but effective methods of recruitment. Other groups are much less well represented among the clergy. It is not sufficient to note with pious surprise that God does not seem to be calling many Afro-Caribbean or Asian Anglicans into ordained ministry in Britain. We need to look at the cultural hurdles that we are placing in their way. *Call to Order* demanded a hard look at the needs of the church nationally and urged a change from a reactive policy of fostering vocations to a proactive one of vigorous recruitment of people gifted to meet the needs.

At this point I would like to revisit the conclusion of the previous section. There I stressed that there is nothing exclusive to ordained ministry that may not be a part of the ministry of the laity. As a result it may look as if the importance of ordination has dwindled away to zero. In fact, as my introduction implied, I value ordination very highly. I simply want to stress that its significance lies in authority and trust rather than the content of the ministry.

> *'Take thou Authority to preach the Word of God and minister the holy Sacraments in the Congregation, where thou shalt be lawfully appointed thereunto.'*

So says the bishop in the ordering of priests in the Book of Common Prayer. At an institution that authority is spelt out with considerable drama. The service is like a covenant – making ceremony between the new incumbent and the existing congregation. Priest and people together promise before the bishop to play their part as different aspects of the ministry of the church are underlined with visible symbols like a door, a stall, a font and bread and wine.

All authority in the church is God's authority; it comes from the 'Author'. Authority for ministry comes from God in three ways. It comes directly from God via the prayer life and spiritual vision of the minister. It comes from below in the respect and trust that the members of the parish invest in their minister. It comes from outside, from peers or bishops as first among equals who support the minister from losing sight of God's mission amid local concerns. The balance between these forms of authority is such an important and delicate one that it becomes the major issue that is consistently keeping our various denominations apart. Catholic, Anglican, Baptist, Reformed, Methodist or charismatic 'New Church', all give some account of how these three sources of authority relate, but the desire to safeguard one form against another creates the differences that have proved to be so intractable. Someone who was suitable for ordination in one denomination might be quite unfit in another because of a mismatch in expectations of how authority was to be exercised in the tradition.

Should Women be Ordained?

It is precisely at this point of authority that the question of how we select people for ministry merges into the question of who should be ordained. Can we identify any category of baptized adults who will never carry the requisite authority and should be excluded from consideration. Each generation in church history has wrestled with various kinds of exclusion. The church has been multicultural since Gentiles were first admitted. Should its leaders in a locality come from the majority rather than minority cultures? Should class and education provide limits? What about handicap? But the most consistent limitation has been the exclusion of women from ordination as presbyter or priest. Some evidence filters through of times when women were ordained (the ecumenical council that ruled against it is evidence of a kind) or of theologians who held their exclusion was a matter of custom rather than principle but until this century most church members have been taught that Christ and his apostles ordained that presbyters be male.

Often the theological arguments have been accompanied by claims of women's biological or psychological inability to carry out tasks of ministry. The most persistent accusation has been of intellectual inferiority, of being unable to distinguish emotive from rational argument. The wealth of examples now available of women succeeding in university education, in business management and in political leadership make this claim less and less plausible.

Systematic studies of gender differences yield some average but not absolute differences in things like muscle power (men are stronger), length of life (women in our society live longer), balance between subjective and objective modes of thinking. None of them add up to any kind of truthful case that women are by their nature unsuitable to exercise authoritative leadership in the church. Plenty of counter-examples exist in this century and a careful look at church history shows that each generation has contained women who were effective and authoritative in their ministry. Like the biblical Deborah, Huldah, Mary Magdalene, Phoebe and Priscilla, they led despite the paucity of official recognition. Their stories are often as briefly told as their biblical counterparts.

While it is clear that some women do emerge into the limelight as good examples and good communicators of the gospel, having authority and commanding respect from men and women in the church, it is not hard to see why many do not. In most cultures the subordination of women to men is a sociological fact which is highlighted in Gen 3 as one of the tragic results of the fall. In her book *Gender and Grace* (IVP, Leicester 1990) Mary van Leeuwen compares the dominion and sociability prescribed for male and female in Gen 1 with a tendency for the male to desire domination and a corresponding desire by the female for social enmeshment described after the entry of sin in Gen 3. We tend to accept subordination in order to achieve community and have much less opportunity to develop confidence in our own intrinsic authority.

I experience this process as I write. A Presbyterian says on the radio, 'The Bible clearly forbids the ordination of women.' I feel my fingers grow heavy at the keys and long to write about a less costly subject. As my example about a community eucharist indicated, the emotional element is as strong amongst men as amongst women. Any compelling argument in favour of women's ordination will be filed under the label 'strident feminism' by some people for whose opinion I care. Perhaps that is why I have filled up most of my allocated word space in this chapter already, leaving room for just the contents of a nutshell.

The argument against the ordination of women is well known. It stresses that Christ was male and that he chose only male apostles. Their letters teach that women should be quiet and submissive in the church. They should not teach or have authority over men. The teaching stems from woman's role at creation which is to be man's helper and submit to his authority as head. Ordaining women disobeys the epistles and contravenes a creation ordinance. It is a departure from the universal faith taught down the centuries.

The case for, being less well known, takes a little longer to outline. It stresses that men and women created in the image of God are equally intended to exercise dominion and bond socially. They are sexually complementary and will always need each other as partners, but loving unity in a life-long partnership does not mean that all the leadership and initiative comes from the male and all the responding and submission comes from the female. The description of sexual love in the Song of Songs presents a much more rounded picture for each of the partners. Apart from this poetic presentation the biblical literature does not attempt to describe differences on which sexual complementarity depends. The biological ones are obvious. Modern studies in human development tend to relate psychological differences to the way in which infants establish their gender identity. Am I the same as the mother to whom I originally bonded at birth or different from her like father? With this may come a predisposition towards bonding and inclusion or towards independence and exclusion. Both qualities are ultimately needed for good leadership.

With the Fall and the entry of sin, marriage and work have become disordered and throughout the Bible the subordination of wives and slaves is a fact which is addressed frequently in parallel. Old Testament laws regulate the worst abuses of both but the gospel looks beyond the limits of a fallen world and declares a new status of wives and slaves in Christ Jesus. The church, however, has to exist in the realities of the world and the epistles urge believers to submit to the existing household hierarchies. With marriage there is an extra creation element which distinguishes it from what is said to slaves. Freedom from the domination of Gen 3 is not freedom to be independent but freedom to be totally one flesh in mutual love.

Paul's argument in 1 Cor 11 is complex because he is

affirming that Christian women have the authority or right (the word has both meanings) to be human beings not sex objects as they pray and prophesy in public worship. At the same time he wants to convince them that the head covering custom is helping to maintain orderly relationships. Long loose hair in that culture is likely to trigger sexual responses. In the politics of sex woman is the image and glory of her man. Paul makes comparisons with other 'head and body' relationships such as God and Christ or Christ and man. The significance in each case is that they are ordered with a 'head' to express unity and love as opposed to independence and rivalry. The ordering does not imply a restriction of ministry and authority. In John's gospel for instance the submission of the Son in the relationship of the Father and Son is stressed precisely because the Son carries out all the same ministry as the Father. We are assured that this is not blasphemous rivalry with God. The mutual love relationship with the Trinity remains secure.

The speaker on the radio might have quoted 1 Tim 2.12 if challenged to support his claim. This comes in a context where heresy and sexual asceticism are two of the apostle's concerns. He wishes to prevent women giving up marriage and child bearing in order to take over ministry roles for which they have not been properly instructed. They should be studying not teaching, learning to submit not trying to dominate. He uses Gen 2 as a parable of Eve falling into error because she had come after Adam and had not been properly instructed. He assured his female readers that they can truly attain salvation following the route of a married sex life and childbearing.

The reader will know that those are not the only possible exegeses of those two difficult passages. Many details in both of them are obscure. They are difficult precisely because the apostles did not see themselves as legislators, laying down the law for all times on this issue. They provide examples of how the new freedom and dignity of the gospel has to be worked out in relation to realities of the fallen world.

The common ground that I share with many opponents of the ordination of women is the deep sadness they feel over the breakdown of long-term marital commitment in our society.

Much fear exists in the relationships between men and women in a fallen world. We know more than any other generation about the mechanics of human development and the way in which security, confidence, achievement and ability to form loving relationships with the opposite sex is nurtured by loving attention from both parents and the strength of the one flesh bond between the parents. Yet somehow the more we know it the less as a society we are actually giving it to our children. The answer does not lie with simple formulas about stay-at-home mothers and absentee commuting fathers. It does not lie with women returning to a picture of feminity as subservient and inferior which is partly self fulfilling but which all women know deep down is untrue to what they are. The real social changes in women's lives brought about by contraception, over-population and greater life expectancy mean that there is plenty of time for childbearing and for substantial full-time ministry as well.

As the last century was the time for taking a Christian stance and working for a social change in relation to slavery so in the late twentieth century it is the time for men and women to affirm one another's authority in ministry. We need to work hard together for partnership which will produce homes where the next generation is loved and secure and fellowships where single people are welcome too.

Note

1. 1 Corinthians 7.20 is the only place where a noun meaning calling appears to be used meaning career or life's work. Gordon Fee suggests Paul intends a double nuance. Christians should live out their calling to Christ in the situation (calling) where they were when God called them. See G. D. Fee *The First Epistle to the Corinthians* (Eerdmans Grand Rapids 1987).

10. The Ministry of All and the Leadership of Some

A Baptist perspective

Paul Beasley-Murray

To state today that 'ministry' is the prerogative as also the responsibility of all God's people is to state the obvious. The calling of the whole people of God to Christian service is accepted by Christians of all traditions. In the words of the Lima document, 'The Spirit calls people to faith, sanctifies them through many gifts, gives them strength to witness to the Gospel, and empowers them to serve hope and love' (*Baptism, Eucharist and Ministry*, WCC Geneva 1982, 3: this document is henceforward referred to as BEM).

Sadly the implications of the obvious have yet to be taken on board by all. Apparent theological agreement has yet to lead to general practical implementation. More often than not ministry is limited to the few, rather than encouraged to become the responsibility of the many. 'Ministry' is still the most frequently used term for the work of the ordained, as distinct from 'the service to which the whole people of God is called, whether as individuals, as a local community, or as the universal Church' (BEM 7b). 'Ministers' is still the preferred term for the ordained within the Free Churches and is also happily used in this sense too by the Anglican Church. The obvious is clearly still not obvious. Hence the need in this essay on ordination to restate what one would have hoped was the obvious.

1. The Ministry of all God's People

In the first place, all God's people are called to ministry. This doctrine of every-member-ministry is based in the New Testament as a whole, but comes to the fore in particular in Eph 4.11–12, where Paul writes of the Risen Christ: 'It was he who gave some to be apostles, some to be prophets, some to be evangelists, and some to be pastors and teachers, to prepare God's people for works of service' (NIV), or as the RSV puts it 'to equip the saints for the work of ministry'. Ministry for Paul is ministry of the whole people of God – it is not confined to apostles, prophets, evangelists, pastors and teachers. Furthermore, as Eph 4.11–16 makes clear, the body of Christ can only be built up as Christians in general are 'prepared' or 'equipped' for the work of 'ministry'. Indeed one can argue from the word Paul uses here for 'preparing' or 'equipping', that without every member ministry the body of Christ will not function aright. For the Greek word *katartizein* in other contexts is used of the setting of broken bones and the mending of broken nets: i.e. one can infer that where Christians in general are not fulfilling their ministries, the church can be likened to a hopeless cripple or to a fisherman seeking to catch fish with gaping holes in his net! If this is true, then we dare not restrict the calling of the whole people of God to the arena of theological debate.

In line with their calling, all God's people are gifted for ministry. This is the teaching of Paul in Rom 12.4–8 and 1 Cor 12.4–12, as also of Peter in 1 Pet 4.10–12. For example, Paul prefaces the list of gifts in 1 Cor 12.9–10 with the words 'Now to each one the manifestation of the Spirit is given for the common good' (1 Cor 12.7), and concludes 'All these (gifts) are the work of one and the same Spirit, and he gives them to each one, just as he determines' (1 Cor 12.11). In a very real sense, all Christians are 'charismatic'. Hence the need to hear again the words of the Lima document: 'All members are called to discover, with the help of the community, the gifts they have received and to use them for the building up of the Church and for the service of the world to which the Church is sent' (BEM 5).

Within my own denominational setting it is this concept of every-member-ministry, along with the related doctrine of the priesthood of all believers, that lies at the heart of our understanding of congregational government. For over against more hierarchical expressions of the body of Christ found in other sections of the Christian church, the Church Meeting for Baptists 'is the occasion when as individuals and as a community the members submit themselves to the guidance of the Holy Spirit and stand under the judgement of God that they may know what is the mind of Christ' (taken from the 1948 Baptist Union Statement on the Church). Or differently expressed, the Church Meeting is a 'charismatic expression of Christian community, in which gifts of leadership and discernment, of wisdom and of prophecy, are shared, in order that God's people discern the mind of Christ for their life together'.

Similarly it is this radical belief that all God's people are 'ministers' which underlies the frequent Baptist practice of following baptism with the laying-on-of-hands. Here prayer is made that the baptismal candidates be filled afresh with the Spirit of God and be thus empowered for service (see Mt 3.16; Acts 1.8; 8.17). Or as a recent Baptist manual on worship puts it: 'Lord, bless these your servants and strengthen them by your Holy Spirit as we commission them for service in the Church and the world in the name of the Lord Jesus Christ' (*Patterns and Prayers for Christian Worship*, OUP, Oxford 1991, 103). For Baptists the church membership roll is − or at least should be − the 'ministry roll' of the church!

2. The leadership of some

All God's people are called to serve, but not all are called to lead. As Paul so delightfully makes clear in 1 Cor 12,

God gives many and various gifts. 'If they were all one part, where would the body be? As it is, there are many parts, but one body' (1 Cor 12.19,20). Most of God's gifts relate to ministry in general. Some, however, relate to the ministry of leadership in particular. Indeed, it is highly significant that in all three lists of spiritual gifts in Paul's writings the gift of leadership is found. True, the actual term 'leadership' does not always appear in our English translations, but the idea is present.

In Rom 12.8, for instance, Paul writes: 'If it is leadership, let him govern diligently' (NIV). Confusion sometimes arises because in some English versions a somewhat different translation is found: for example, the RSV translates the phrase: 'he who gives aid, with zeal'. In fact the underlying Greek verb can mean both 'to lead' and 'to care for'. However, rather than seeking to make distinctions between these two meanings, it is more helpful to note how the two meanings may interrelate: leadership within a church context is not about the exercise of power, but rather is about the exercise of care.

In 1 Cor 12.8 Paul refers to 'those with gifts of administration'. It is now increasingly recognized that Paul did not have in mind 'secretarial' gifts, so much as leadership gifts. The fact is that the underlying Greek noun literally means 'helmsmanship'. It was a term often used metaphorically in Greek literature of the art of government: the statesman guiding the 'ship of state'. Here in 1 Cor 12, of course, the ship in question is the church. Within the context of every-member ministry there are those specially gifted to 'preside' over the church's life, 'guiding the life of the community in its worship, its mission and its caring ministry' (BEM 13).

The concept of leadership is also present in Paul's third list of spiritual gifts in Eph 4.7–13, where amongst the various 'offices' of ministry is to be found that of the pastor-teacher (note that in the Greek there is only one definite article covering both 'pastors and teachers' which indicates that this is one and the same office). Like all the other offices, in the first place this is an 'enabling' ministry – enabling the people of God to fulfil their ministry. However, the actual term 'pastor' would also have carried clear overtones of leadership, for in the ancient world the word 'pastor' or 'shepherd' was often used as a synonym for a 'leader' or 'king'.

With such Scriptural precedent in mind, it seems fair to argue that this concept of leadership is the distinguishing concept between the ordained ministry of the church and the general ministry of the church. How that leadership will be exercised will vary. Its content however will include in particular the preaching and teaching of God's Word (Eph 4.11; 1 Tim 3.2: cf also Acts 6.4), the oversight of God's people (Acts 20.28; 1 Pet 5.2), and the equipping of God's people for service (Eph 4.11,12). An evangelistic thrust will also be a mark of such a ministry (2 Tim 4.5). But none of these specific tasks of teaching, pastoral care, evangelism, and enabling, are exclusive to the ordained. Indeed, in any given local church it would be exceedingly limiting if, for instance, pastoral care and evangelism were to be the exclusive preserve of the pastor alone − if a church is to grow and develop, such tasks need to be shared. However, as the overall leader of a church the ordained 'minister' is responsible for ensuring that these tasks are responsibly delegated. Leadership is the distinguishing mark of the ordained.

Does this therefore mean to say that the ordained are the only leaders in a local church? Hopefully not. Leadership is a task to be shared. In the New Testament church, for instance, there was always a plurality of leadership (see, for instance, Acts 13.1; 14.231 15.23; 20.17,28; Phil 1.1). The New Testament knows nothing of the kind of one-man ministry (the so-called 'monarchical espiscopate'!) still so prevalent in many churches today. Or rather, the only example of a one-man ministry in the New Testament is found in 3 Jn 9, where Diotrophes 'who loves to be first' is no example to be followed, but a warning to be taken note of. Likewise in today's churches leadership should always be corporate. It matters not what the nomenclature of the leadership team be − whether the leaders be termed 'deacons' or 'elders', 'stewards' or 'the oversight' − the important thing is that there be such people who share in the task of leadership, giving oversight and direction to the ongoing life and mission of the church.

The question immediately arises as to what then is the distinction between such leaders and the ordained. If leadership is shared, then how may one leader be distinguished from another? Are the ordained leaders to be distinguished from other leaders within the church on the grounds of the training they have received? Clearly training is crucial — the ability to handle God's Word knowledgeably and to reflect theologically upon issues facing the church is of major importance. First and foremost, however, the distinction is to be found not within education and preparation for ministry, but rather in calling and function: the ordained person (the 'pastor' or whatever the appropriate term may be) is called to be the leader of the leaders. As in the Jerusalem church James exercised the role of the presiding elder, so in today's churches ordained ministers are called to exercise 'presidency', and in this way spearhead the life and mission of the church. (In the case of a church enjoying the services of more than one ordained person, then the ordained will form a leadership team within the team). However, in today's context there is a further distinction related to this very function. Over against the locally-recognized ministry of deacons and elders and other leaders, the ministry of the ordained is nationally recognized. The former enjoy the recognition and trust of their local church, the latter have been accorded recognition and trust by the wider church as also by the local church. This wider recognition and trust come in to particular focus within the service of ordination itself, and result in enrolment on the particular denomination's list of accredited ministers.

Within my own denomination many Baptist churches today recognize the particular ministry of deacons and elders by appointing them with prayer and with the laying on of hands. Thus *Patterns and Prayers for Christian Worship* 168–170 provides an order of service for a 'commissioning of local church workers' (i.e. deacons and elders), which it believes to be 'appropriate when the church meeting has previously called a person to a position of leadership and responsibility'.

However, unlike ordination, this commissioning service is very much an act of the local church. (So far I have described the present practice of Baptists within the Baptist Union of Great Britain. Amongst Baptists in the USA, however, it is normal for deacons to be 'ordained' – and for their ordination to be accepted when they move to other churches).

In ordination recognition and trust are formally accorded to the ordinand by the wider church. It marks the culmination of a fairly lengthy period of testing and training, and is the occasion when churches together publicly recognize certain individuals as called of God to exercise leadership among them, and through the laying on of hands and prayer ask that God will fill them afresh with his Spirit as they embark upon this new stage of their Christian service (see Acts 6.1–11; 13.1–3; 1 Tim 4.14). Although in a British Baptist context such a service of ordination normally takes place in a local church, ordination is never just an act of the local church. Precisely because ordination involves national recognition, the wider church is always present through its representatives. For British Baptists, at the very least both the local association of churches as also the Baptist Union is represented in the act of ordination.

The leadership of both men and women It is important to stress that leadership gifts are not restricted to men. The Scriptures teach that the Spirit gives his gifts irrespective of gender (Acts 2.17,18). Although certain cultural situations might have limited leadership to men (see 1 Cor 11.3–6; 14.33–36; 1 Tim 2.11–15), in principle there is no Scriptural reason why women should not share in the leadership. Just as in the church in Rome women took the lead (see Rom 16.1–2,3,7 where Paul mentions Phoebe the deacon, Prisca the teacher, and Junia the apostle), so also may they today. The presumed superiority of male over female no longer exists in Christ (Gal 3.28). In Christ a new order has come into being. Women can and should expect to be playing varying roles within Christian leadership.

BEM 18 unfortunately sits on the fence and instead of making specific recommendations in favour of the ordination of women, prefers to recognize that there are differences between the churches on this particular issue. In England today the Anglican church is divided over this issue. Strangely, however, the Church of England is happy with women deacons, whose ministry could be deemed illegitimate in the light of those passages traditionally cited in favour of male leadership: instead, the arguments appear to be far more concerned with traditions relating to priesthood and the eucharist, which from a Free Church perspective have no foundation in Scripture!

3. The Ministry of all and the Leadership of Some: the Consequences

If we are right in our understanding of the teaching of the Scriptures on the ministry of all and the leadership of some, then this means that much of the mystique that over the centuries has built up around ordination ought to be eliminated. Indeed, a fairly radical shift needs to take place in the church, if the church is to begin to operate on New Testament principles.

a) Ordination is not to the ministry In the first place, there should be a recognition that ordination is never to 'the ministry' as such. In this respect the Oxford English Dictionary is wrong: ordination is not the 'appointment or admission to the ministry of the church', as though pastoral leadership were *the* ministry. For, as has already been argued, ministry is not the exclusive preserve of some, but is rather the duty and responsibility of all God's people. In many ways the present use of the term 'minister' is unfortunate. All God's people are ministers. It would be a far healthier witness to the New Testament understanding of the church if 'ministers' were known by the functional term 'pastor'. True, there are difficulties in such nomenclature. The term 'pastor' has tended to be used of those who have not been formally trained – in Baptist churches, for instance, we have talked of 'lay pastors', while 'ministers' have been 'the professionals'. Furthermore, it could be argued that the term 'pastor' is a hang-over from a rural society, and sounds strange in today's largely urban world. Would the phrase 'pastoral leader' be an improvement?

It is because all God's people are called to ministry, that the use of such terms as 'clergy' and 'laity' are equally incorrect and unhelpful. By definition, those called to exercise pastoral leadership within the churches are themselves members of God's 'laos', i.e. they too belong to the people of God. This being the case, we should cease to use the term 'lay' within the Christian church. Similarly distinctive clerical dress – whether cassock and bands or simply a clerical collar – should be questioned. For on the whole clerical dress creates and maintains a false distinction between the ordained and the non-ordained. True, it could be argued that in certain situations some kind of distinctive 'uniform' is helpful – e.g. within the context of a hospital or industrial chaplaincy. But these advantages are dubious. The image of special status is reinforced, and the ministry of other Christians is minimised. If a badge is needed, what is wrong with a cross – if necessary, a sizeable wooden cross worn around the neck? Certainly the 'dressing up' that has been the hallmark of the Anglican and Roman Catholic churches gives the impression of effeminacy, and lends conviction to the underlying feeling that the 'clergy' do not belong to the real world.

Likewise, the use of the title 'Reverend' is thoroughly inappropriate, let alone such titles as 'Right Reverend' and 'Most Reverend', or indeed 'His Grace'. A pastor may be worthy of respect, but surely not of 'reverence'. False distinctions are being created. At the very least, within the church context the title 'Reverend' should be done away with. As far as public life is concerned, we may still have to continue with the use of this term, since it has come to be perceived as a mark of one who is deemed as professionally competent by their peers!

b) Ordination does not involve metamorphosis Here is yet another consequence of a biblical understanding of ministry and leadership. Through the laying-on-of-hands the ordinand does not become another person, as if another step within the evolutionary process has been reached. Pastors are not brought nearer to God as a consequence of the rite of ordination. There are no first or second class citizens within the kingdom of God. All God's people are called to be men and women of God.

On the other hand, in order to fulfil their role as leaders of the people of God, pastors do have a special responsibility to develop their relationship with their Lord (see Acts 20.28). Neglect of this relationship negates their ministry. For very practical reasons, pastors need to practise what they preach, for otherwise their pastoral authority will be totally undermined. Hence in many ordination rituals ordinands are asked to commit themselves afresh to daily prayer and a daily reading of the Scriptures. However, the living of a holy life is not dependent upon ordination, nor is it an inevitable consequence of ordination. Those who have been ordained still belong to the human race!

Ordination is primarily about recognition and trust. It is not a means of special grace, conferring upon the ordinand some new status. At the most ordination is a special means of grace, in the sense that it is the occasion when prayer is made that God may bless his servants with the infilling and empowering of his Holy Spirit (see 1 Tim 4.1). This blessing, however, is not to be confined to the day of ordination − for the blessing that is sought is the blessing on all the years of service that lie ahead.

c) Ordination is not indelible If ordination is primarily functional, and has more to do with role than with status, then it is possible for that function to be given up. Ordination cannot therefore be indelible, in the sense that it is for life. Once a 'minister', one is not necessarily a 'minister' for ever. In cost effective terms it may make sense for ordination to be viewed for life, but there is no New Testament warrant for this understanding. There may well be circumstances, positive or negative, which may lead a pastor to believe it right to withdraw from leadership. Having said that, BEM 48 is surely correct in stating: 'Initial commitment to ordained ministry ought normally to be made without reserve or time limit'.

166

Unfortunately there is a tendency on the part of some to equate being taken off their denomination's accredited list of 'ministers' with being struck off the Medical Register or being defrocked. Removal from such an accredited list is often unnecessarily associated with guilt and failure. This need not be the case. Ordination need not be for life.

d) Ordination is not an initiation into priesthood Ordination does not lead to ordinands exercising some peculiarly priestly role of their own, but rather they share with all God's people in the corporate priesthood of all believers (1 Pet 2 4,9). Strangely BEM contradicts itself on this point. It begins by rightly recognizing that 'the New Testament never uses the term "priesthood" or "priest" to designate the ordained ministry or ordained minister', but rather reserves the term 'on the one hand for the unique priesthood of Jesus Christ and, on the other hand, for the royal and prophetic priesthood of all baptized' (BEM Commentary on 17). However, on the basis of later church usage BEM argues that the ordained 'may appropriately be called priests because they fulfil a particular priestly service by strengthening and building up the royal and prophetic priesthood of the faithful through word and sacraments, through their prayers of intercession, and through their pastoral guidance of the community' (BEM 17). This argument creates unhelpful and untrue distinctions between the ordained and the nonordained. None of the tasks included in BEM's definition of the service of the ordained is necessarily exclusive to the ordained.

There are no biblical grounds for the Roman Catholic understanding of the priesthood in terms of special authority to celebrate the mass. Furthermore, there are no biblical grounds for the Reformed understanding of ordination as a setting aside of a person to 'the ministry of word and sacraments'. For although the 'ministry of the word' is a vital and important part of any pastor's calling, there is nothing to indicate that this is an exclusive calling. Likewise, although in most church situations the pastor will normally participate in the baptizing and preside at the Lord's Table, neither ordinance is the pastor's exclusive preserve. Where the pastor baptizes or presides at the Lord's Table, the pastor does so, not by virtue of being a priest mediating between God and his people, but by virtue of being the recognized and trusted leader of God's flock. Indeed, there is no Scriptural reason why anyone may not perform either function provided it is at the invitation of the church.Because of the biblical doctrine of the priesthood of all believers, it is important that churches do not encourage any false sacerdotalism. In this regard the practice in British Baptist churches, for instance, of asking the newly ordained pastor to pronounce a blessing at the end of an ordination service is unhelpful, for it gives the impression that ordination has conferred special powers upon the ordinand. Likewise, any tendency to encourage the newly ordained pastor to preside at a celebration of the Lord's Supper *within the context of ordination* is to be resisted – for again the impression is given that through ordination a special priestly status has been received through the act of laying-on-of-hands.

4. The Call to Leadership: a Precondition of Ordination

Ordination presupposes the call of God. Indeed, ordination is the occasion when the church recognizes God's prior call upon the life of the ordinand. The question, however, arises: how is that call recognized? Of what does a call to leadership consist?

The call to leadership amongst the people of God is, in fact, made up of a number of components:

First, the call needs to be sensed within the life of the individual. However, just as there is no stereotyped conversion experience, so too there is no fixed pattern of call. A call, for instance, need not be dramatic in nature – the experience of Isaiah in the temple is no more typical of a call than is the experience of Paul on the Damascus Road typical of conversion. In other words, 'people are called in differing ways to the ordained ministry . . . This call may be discerned through personal prayer and reflection, as well as through suggestion, example, encouragement, guidance . . .' (BEM 45). Nonetheless, common to all those called of God to leadership among his people will be a sense of inward constraint (1 Cor 9.16) and a real desire to serve the Lord in such a way (1 Tim 3.1).

Secondly, the call will be evidenced by appropriate gifts for such leadership. In order to lead God's people, the ordinand will need to be able to communicate effectively (1 Tim 3.2) and relate helpfully with others (1 Tim 3.3). An ability to think and a facility for self-awareness, are equally vital.

Thirdly, the call will be evidenced by character (cf 1 Tim 3.1–7). Love, humility, holiness, industry, perseverance — such characteristics are essential for Christian leadership. It cannot be sufficiently stressed that the test of character is fundamental to the call of God. Gifts without character are worthless. The ordinand's life, therefore, must be marked by spiritual authenticity discernible both within and without the church (see 1 Tim 3.7).

Fourthly, the genuineness of the call must be recognized by the people of God. It is not enough for an individual to feel convinced. As BEM rightly states: 'This call must be authenticated by the Church's recognition of the gifts and graces of the particular person, both natural and spiritually given, needed for the ministry to be performed' (BEM 45). Such objective recognition may at times precede the subjective call within the life of the individual, in the sense that on occasion individuals within the church may take the initiative and share their conviction that God is indeed calling a particular individual to leadership among his people (see Acts 13.1–3). In today's context, however, it is usually the potential ordinand who submits a subjective sense of call to the scrutiny of others. In the first place it surely is right that this call be tested by the local church of which the potential ordinand is a member.

Fifthly, the call should be further tested by the wider church. Precisely how this is done will vary from denomination to denomination. Within a British Baptist context, this is first done by the local association of churches through its ministerial

169

recognition committee, and then normally through a Baptist college, which in its acceptance procedures tests the call on behalf of the Baptist Union.

Sixthly, as part of the ongoing testing process, the ordinand will receive training. For gifts need to be developed, character needs to be formed, the mind needs to be stretched and informed, practical ministry skills need to be learned. Training is not just desirable, it is necessary, if competent leadership is to be exercised amongst God's people today. While the precise form of this training may vary from person to person, candidates will 'need appropriate preparation through study of scripture and theology, prayer and spirituality, and through acquaintance with the social and human realities of the contemporary world' (BEM 47). In other words, a purely academic theological education is insufficient. 'Ministerial formation', as it is called, is a broader exercise.

Seventhly, final confirmation of the call is gained when the ordinand receives and accepts the call from a local congregation of God's people to exercise pastoral leadership amongst them.

5. The Public Recognition of Leadership: the Service of Ordination

The precise form of such a service will no doubt vary from church to church, and denomination to denomination. However, within a service of ordination, the following actions would appear desirable:

First, the nature of ordination and of the task involved in leadership amongst God's people should be made plain. On an occasion when the particular ministry of a person (or persons) is in view, it is important that the congregation is reminded that all God's people are called to ministry. Indeed, it would be good if an opportunity might be given for the congregation to reaffirm their commitment to Christ and the ministries to which he has called them.

Secondly, a series of brief statements should be included in which the preconditions relating to ordination are seen to be fulfilled. Within my own denomination, where generally people are ordained on an individual basis within their local church, it would be normal, for instance, for ordinands to affirm their belief that God has called them to be leaders in his church; for the 'sending' church from which they come to tell how they were led to recognize the call and commend the ordinand for training, for the 'calling' church to tell how they were led to issue an invitation to the ordinand to be their pastor.

Thirdly, an opportunity should be given for ordinands to reaffirm their faith in the Gospel of Jesus Christ and to publicly commit themselves to the task of pastoral leadership.

Fourthly, the actual ordination needs to be seen not as an action of a particular person (a bishop or a college principal, for example), but rather an action of the whole church. Lest misunderstanding occur and the impression be given that in ordination a particular grace is conferred from one person to another, it is important that more than one individual is involved in the laying on of hands, and that not all of those sharing in that ceremony be ordained themselves. A variety of representatives should share in the ordination. Thus within my own denomination, it would be customary for representatives of the sending and calling churches, as also of the local association of churches and of the wider Baptist Union, to take part in the laying-on-of-hands. Indeed, there is much to be said for ensuring that prayers for the ordinand are not limited to the presiding 'minister' – normally an ordained person (although there is no reason why this should have to be so) – but rather that several people, ordained and non-ordained, lead God's people in brief prayers, in which God's blessing is sought on the ordinand as also a fresh empowering and filling of the Spirit, and in this way make clear that ordination is no priestly activity but rather a church activity. Certainly, there are no Scriptural grounds for ordination being viewed as an exclusively episcopal activity (pace BEM 52); if the doctrine of apostolic succession is to be found in Scripture at all, then it relates to the faithful transmission of the Word by the continuing apostolic community (2 Tim 2.2) rather than to a class of specially authorized ministers. (Indeed, this is not simply a theological truth, but also a historical truth: the apostolic doctrine and ministry have sometimes been maintained by the members of the church more clearly than by their ordained leaders).

Fifthly, at the conclusion of the ordination it is good to present to ordinands a Bible, as a sign of their authority, which in turn is a reminder that pastor and people alike are all under the authority of the Word of God.

6. Leadership Amongst God's People: Developments Subsequent to Ordination

Ordination marks a new stage of Christian service. Although the ordinand may have already shared in the leadership of a local church – perhaps as a deacon or as an elder or as a house group leader – in ordination the ordinand is given a new responsibility to lead the people of God forward in its worship, fellowship and mission to the world. Such a responsibility inevitably brings with it a certain amount of authority. Indeed, the church through the very act of ordination entrusts the ordinand with power to lead. This power, however, is limited. For, following the pattern of the Servant-King, such leadership will always be non-coercive (see 1 Pet 5.2–3). Leadership may therefore be authoritative, but never authoritarian. People must always be free to accept or not to accept the direction offered by their leaders. On the other hand, where there is recognition of and trust in a leader's calling, there all necessary authority for pastoral leadership will be found. Such recognition and trust, however, although present within an ordination service, can never be taken for granted; they have to be repeatedly won. Ultimately people follow their leaders not because of their 'office', but rather because they discern within them the marks of Christian leadership.

From a Baptist perspective it is important to stress that although in ordination the ordinand is given recognition by the wider church, the ordinand is not thereby created a representative of the wider church. The local church is always

172

the representative of the wider church (see 1 Cor 1.2). Where in the community the pastor is called to represent the local or wider church, such representation is always on behalf of the local or wider church. There are no biblical grounds for asserting that the ordained 'provide a focus of its (the church's) unity' (pace BEM 8).

Hopefully ordination does not mark the end of personal growth and development, but rather should always lead to an ongoing commitment to study God's Word and to a continual updating of ministry skills. Ordination may mark the end of initial training, but not the end of theological development and learning. In a rapidly changing world, leaders of God's people cannot afford to stand still in their thinking. If their leadership is to be creative and responsive to the new challenges which society constantly poses to the church, then they too need to be given regular opportunities to reflect and to develop themselves.

Ordination in the first place normally leads to pastoral oversight of a local church. However, the ministry of the ordained need not be limited to a local church. A wider ministry of pastoral leadership may be exercised in and on behalf of the churches – whether in a denominational or ecumenical appointment.

Although for the most part ordination leads to fulltime paid ministry, this is not a necessary concomitant. As BEM 46 states, 'the church may also ordain people who remain in other occupations or employment'. The apostle Paul himself at times exercised a tent-making ministry! Indeed, in an increasingly missionary situation, where churchplanting may become the norm rather than the exception, tent-making ministries may well increase.

In conclusion

There is no ministry in the church more important than that of pastoral leadership. We do, however, no favours to that ministry if we allow it to become encumbered with all kinds of unhelpful and indeed un-biblical practices. For the sake of effective ministry and mission the undergrowth of sentiment and tradition needs to be cleared, in order to free not only the people of God in general for their various ministries, but also the ordained for their particular ministry. Only where the ministry of all and the leadership of some is a reality can we expect the church to grow and develop.